The EDEN DIET

The EDEN DIET

You Can **Eat** Treats, **Enjoy** Your Food, *and* **Lose** Weight

Rita Hancock, MD

ZONDERVAN.com/
AUTHOR**TRACKER**
follow your favorite authors

ZONDERVAN

The Eden Diet
Copyright © 2010 by Rita M. Hancock

This title is also available as a Zondervan ebook. Visit www.zondervan.com/ebooks.

This title is also available in a Zondervan audio edition. Visit www.zondervan.fm.

Requests for information should be addressed to:

Zondervan, *Grand Rapids, Michigan 49530*

Library of Congress Cataloging-in-Publication Data

Hancock, Rita M.
    The Eden diet : how to eat treats, enjoy your food, and lose weight / Rita M.
Hancock. — [Rev. ed.].
      p. cm.
    Includes bibliographical references.
    ISBN 978-0-310-32808-7
    1. Reducing diets. 2. Weight loss — Religious aspects — Christianity. I. Title.
RM222.2H227 2009
  613.2'5 — dc22   2009041410

Scripture taken from the Holy Bible, *Today's New International Version*™. *TNIV*®. Copyright © 2001, 2005 by Biblica, Inc.™ Used by permission of Zondervan. All rights reserved worldwide.

Scripture quotations marked NIV are taken from the Holy Bible, *New International Version*®, *NIV*®. Copyright © 1973, 1978, 1984 by Biblica, Inc.™ Used by permission of Zondervan. All rights reserved worldwide.

Scripture quotations marked AMP are taken from *The Amplified Bible.* Copyright © 1954, 1958, 1962, 1964, 1965, 1987 by The Lockman Foundation. All rights reserved. Used by permission.

Scripture quotations marked KJV are taken from the King James Version of the Bible.

Cover design: Michelle Lenger
Interior design: Beth Shagene

Printed in the United States of America

11 12 13 14 15 16 • 25 24 23 22 21 20 19 18 17 16 15 14 13 12 11 10 9 8 7 6 5 4 3

Contents

Introduction 7

Part One
A New Paradigm for Weight Loss

1. Overview of the Eden Diet 21
2. Say Good-Bye to the Diet Mentality 33
3. There Is No Bad Food 57

Part Two
The Eden Diet: How to Get Skinny Eating Normal Food

4. Rediscover Your Hunger Signals 81
5. Less Food, More Joy. 109
6. The Eden Diet in Action 127

Part Three
How to Beat Temptation

7. Feed Emotional Hunger the Right Way 149
8. Temptation-Fighting Tools. 177
9. Press On. 193

Conclusion 201
Appendix A: Eating Disorders 204
Appendix B: Time Management for Weight Loss 207
Appendix C: Prayers 209
Appendix D: Scriptural Tools 212
Appendix E: FAQs 215
Notes 219
Additional Help 223

My Prayer

Dear Lord,

I pray that you will help me surrender to your divine guidance, not only in the area of my disordered eating habits, but also in all aspects of my life. I pray that you gently and mercifully break down my barriers to better health, whether the barriers are mistaken beliefs about food, eating, dieting, and exercise; conscious or unconscious unhealthy eating habits; or sin. I ask that you forgive my sins, give me victory over them, and enable me to succeed not only in the area of improving my health but also in all areas of my life.

You, Lord, are my inheritance. You are my food and drink, my highest joy.

Amen.

Introduction

Have you ever wondered what your life might have been like if Adam and Eve hadn't eaten the forbidden fruit? Think about it. If they hadn't disobeyed God and gotten us kicked out of the garden, perhaps we'd have been able to live there with them.

In paradise everything would have been easier—even weight control.

If we had lived in Eden, we would have eaten only when we were hungry, and we would have eaten less. Therefore, we would have automatically reached our ideal weight without trying.

Instead of food being the center of our universe, God would have been the center. We wouldn't even have thought about food until we felt hungry. That's right—we would have eaten primarily for sustenance and in response to our God-given internal hunger signals, not to escape boredom or to fill our emotional or spiritual voids.

And we would have eaten any food that was readily available without regard to whether it was good or bad for us. We wouldn't have had consciences about such things.

If, on occasion, we ate rich, high-calorie foods like honey, nuts, fatty meats, or dairy products, we would have done so without guilt. We wouldn't have worried about being too fat, and we wouldn't have felt the need to pay penance for our fatness by being on a perpetual diet.

Regarding exercise, we would have expended energy the natural way—by walking and working and looking after the garden. It wouldn't have been a chore to exercise, and we wouldn't have done it to make up for overeating. We would have exercised simply as a means to an end and also because it felt good. It would have been a way to worship God with our bodies.

Wouldn't it be great if we could go back to that pure, uncorrupted way of thinking—or should I say not thinking—about weight control? What if we could just listen to our bodies' internal cues, eat only when we're truly hungry, eat less, and enjoy any food God provided without guilt? And what if we could once again think of exercise as being fun, as we did when we were kids? Or, at least, think of it as an act of worship?

We could be free from bondage to what we should or shouldn't eat, free from concerns about body image, and we'd be overflowing with the joy and peace of God. And we'd be thinner and healthier *without trying*.

Eden Was How It Could Have Been, but This Is How It Is

Many of us disregard or have never realized that God gave us hunger pangs for a reason: so that we would experience them. Instead, we eat incredibly large portions of food, and we eat so frequently that we rarely feel hungry. We eat *ahead* of our hunger rather than behind it.

Usually we eat for reasons external to our stomach, such as emotional, intellectual, or sinful reasons (the sight of food, the smell of food, depression, anxiety, stress, boredom, and greed). Or we eat according to the clock. We say, "It's time to eat," without even stopping to consider what our internal signals might say.

If we checked with our internal signals before eating, most of the time they'd say, "What? You don't need food yet."

In addition to having forgotten to use our hunger pangs, we also have another barrier to losing weight: when God put us in the garden of Eden, fattening food was harder to come by.

In the garden, if you wanted honey, you would have had to steal it from bees (which have stingers), so you probably would have thought twice about eating it. To get nuts, you would have had to collect them and crack open the shells with rocks (which would be painstaking work).

If you had any sense, you probably would have said, "Uhh ... never mind about that honey up in that bee hive. I think I'll just eat this green pepper and these berries right in front of me."

Even if you decided to go for the less healthy foods, you would have listened to the inner wisdom God gave you and eaten only a small portion — just enough to quiet the hunger pangs so you could get back to thinking about God.

By contrast, now it's easy and relatively inexpensive to get fattening food served in huge portions. You can have a large four-meat, extra-cheese pizza delivered to your home in thirty minutes or less. You can pick up an enormous fast-food cheeseburger combo meal in three minutes at the drive-through. Or you can microwave a grande burrito in thirty seconds at the convenience store.

Ironically, if you want to prepare a healthy homemade meal like a stir-fry, or even meatloaf, mashed potatoes, and vegetables, it might take you a couple hours.

And consider how we are tempted by food advertisements. They're everywhere — on billboards, in magazines, in television and radio commercials, in pictures on the sides of delivery trucks, on Internet ads, and in coupon mailers that come to our homes. We're constantly bombarded with reminders to eat, usually when we're not actually hungry.

To top it all off, we have become exceedingly lazy. In the beginning, we had no choice but to exercise. Now we have labor-saving devices like automobiles, elevators, and washing machines that on the one hand help us but on the other hand hurt us. They allow us to expend less energy and gain excess weight.

Should it be a surprise that we become more overweight and miserable with each passing year? We're doing everything opposite to the way God intended.

Can You Relate?

If you have a weight problem, do you eat in such a way that you rarely feel hunger? Perhaps you eat because of the time on the clock, completely disconnected from your internal compass—your God-given hunger pangs. Or you eat in response to the sight, smell, or taste of food when you're not hungry.

Perhaps you only feel hunger when you're dieting, and then, when you go off the diet, you stop feeling hungry because you go back to eating according to external cues. So you regain all the weight you lost on the diet—and more—which leads to more depression and more emotional eating.

Maybe you're so overcommitted in your schedule that you have no time to eat properly. You have to eat fattening take-out food several nights a week.

Or maybe your extensive to-do list distracts you while you eat and causes you to shovel in extra food without realizing it. It's no wonder you think you eat like a bird yet still gain weight. You eat mindlessly.

What about exercise? Do you think of it as a painful chore? Or do you enjoy moving around as you did when you were a kid?

If I just described you, don't worry. It's never too late to change. As you continue to read *The Eden Diet*, you will learn to submit your flawed attitudes and habits to God so you can receive a renewed mind as well as a transformed body, just as Paul talked about in Romans 12:1–2:

> Therefore, I urge you, brothers and sisters, in view of God's mercy, to offer your bodies as a living sacrifice, holy and pleasing to God—this is true worship. Do not conform to the pattern of this world, but be transformed by the renew-

ing of your mind. Then you will be able to test and approve what God's will is—his good, pleasing and perfect will.

Just as a dog shakes off water, you'll shake off the fattening lies about weight control that the world has brainwashed you with. Then you'll replace those lies with God's amazingly simple truth for how to lose weight: follow the hunger-pang system he gave you in the beginning.

Doesn't it make more sense to cooperate with God's system than to fight against it?

We Must Change Our Ways before It's Too Late

The prevalence of obesity in the US is climbing at an alarming rate. In 1991, no state had an obesity rate above 20 percent. However, in 2009, two-thirds of the states reported obesity rates greater than 25 percent, and four states reported rates of over 30 percent.[1]

What does that mean in terms of actual pounds? According to the National Center for Health Statistics, adults are, on average, twenty-five pounds heavier than similarly aged adults were in 1960.[2]

I assume you know that obesity is dangerous to your health, but I wonder if you know the full extent of it. Obesity causes high blood pressure, cardiovascular disease, diabetes, obstructive sleep apnea, gallstones, and cancer, including breast, endometrial, prostate, and colon cancers. In fact, it will probably kill you one day if you don't change your ways, as obesity contributes to more than four hundred thousand deaths in the United States annually.

Even if obesity doesn't directly kill you, it will probably still ruin your life if you don't do something about it. Carrying around excess weight causes premature wear and tear on the joints, which in turn causes severe pain and disability.

And it limits you from engaging in the activities you enjoy. If you can't fit into the airplane seat or the movie theater seat, or if you can't walk because of knee or back pain, you take fewer vacations and engage in fewer social events. Then you become socially isolated and even more miserable and depressed.

We must do what it takes to improve our eating and exercise habits, not only for our own sake, but also for the sake of future generations. Over the next several decades, the life expectancy for the average American child is projected to shorten by five years because of the obesity epidemic, according to a report published in the *New England Journal of Medicine*.[3]

Did you get that? I said your children and grandchildren might die five years earlier because of their eating habits. Now are you ready to set a better example for them? I assume you are, or you wouldn't be reading this book.

What Do I Know About Weight Control?

I'm a medical doctor. Specifically, I'm a physical medicine and rehabilitation specialist with subspecialty board certification in pain management. That means I help people achieve optimal physical functioning after illness or injury. Part of my job is to help my patients lose weight in order to take pressure off of their painful joints.

I received my medical degree from the State University of New York at Buffalo, completed an internship in internal medicine at Baylor University Medical Center in Dallas, and completed a residency in physical medicine and rehabilitation at the University of Texas Southwestern Medical Center in Dallas.

In addition to those credentials, I have specialized knowledge about weight control. As an undergraduate at Cornell University, I minored in nutrition, completed a thesis on the control of body weight, and participated in obesity research under the guidance of a leading world researcher on obesity.

In medical school I was awarded two research fellowships. One was the American Gastroenterologic Association Medical Student Research Fellowship to study digestive diseases, and the other was the prestigious National Institute of Health Medical Student Research

Training Fellowship. That allowed me the great privilege to study at the Center for Human Nutrition in Dallas, Texas, for two full years, under the mentorship of several world leaders in the areas of fat metabolism and nutrition.

I have yet another kind of weight-control education that perfectly qualifies me to write this book. In a way, it's the only part of my education I wish I *didn't* have: I grew up morbidly obese. I know from firsthand experience what it's like to suffer with—and then overcome—a serious weight problem.

As far back as I can remember I weighed double what the other kids weighed. By the time I was seventeen years old I was 5'1", weighed 207 pounds, and wore a tight size 20 jeans. My thighs were as big around as my waist is today.

As a junior in high school, I decided I'd had enough. I was tired of being made fun of, and I was tired of feeling self-conscious and miserable all the time. So I lost weight: seventy-five pounds, to be exact.

As you might expect, the weight loss completely transformed my body. However, it did little to change the underlying thoughts and attitudes about food that led to my obesity in the first place. I still had to undergo a mental transformation. Otherwise, I was going to gain that weight right back.

Eventually God showed me that the secret to weight control was as simple as looking inward—to the programming he'd given me in the beginning: my hunger pangs. He helped me identify my hunger pangs and use them as a compass to guide my eating.

Next he revealed why I gained the weight as a child. I had unconscious programming, automatic habits, and a sin nature that compelled me to eat for all the wrong reasons. Finally, he gave me practical tools that allowed me to resist the urge to eat when I wasn't hungry, even when faced with the greatest of temptations.

In the following chapters, I discuss the practical weight-loss insights and tools that God gave me. That way you can apply them effectively in your own life and achieve the slimmer, healthier body God intended for you to have in the beginning.

One Diet Fits All?

The Eden Diet is for people who want to break free from bondage to food and eating. It's for those who seek to make Christ (not food) the Lord of their lives. It's for those who wish to lose weight and become healthier in all dimensions (mind, body, and spirit). And it's for those who want to experience the fruits of the Spirit—peace, love, and joy—rather than strife.

But, the Eden Diet is not right for everybody. I don't believe in one-size-fits-all treatment. Obesity and eating disorders come about for many different reasons and therefore need to be treated in unique ways, depending on the individual.

Even if there were only one cause for obesity, different people would still require different treatment. There are at least twenty different anti-inflammatory medicines for osteoarthritis. It follows logically that different people need different dietary solutions for weight loss, as well.

Just as I don't expect my book to help everybody, I don't expect everyone to agree with me philosophically. *The Eden Diet* will not appeal to people of all religions. Though all people are invited to read it if they're interested, it's intended primarily for an adult Christian readership. If you are opposed to the message of Christianity, you should probably put this book down and read one of the many secular books that tout a similar anti-dieting philosophy for weight loss.

What if you are a Christian but are appalled by the idea of eating processed or fattening food in moderation? You can't understand how I, as a medical doctor, could advocate eating anything other than something 100 percent perfectly healthy. If you're an extremely healthy eater, please don't hurl stones at me because of my message. With all due respect, remember that not everyone is like you. Some people have emotional reasons for overeating; still others have eating disorders.

Please don't misunderstand. I love to eat vegetables. They truly nourish your body. It's just that I wish people wouldn't have philosophical food fights over which foods are right or wrong to eat. Doing so just causes people strife and distracts them from Christ, just as it did back in the days when people argued about whether it was right to eat meat that had been offered to idols.

My Christian Beliefs

I believe that God is love; everything he does is rooted in his love for you, and he is merciful, slow to anger, and quick to forgive. He wants desperately for you to repent and return to him, no matter what you did that caused your separation from him. He does not condemn you if you eat in a way that some people would call "wrong." So, nobody else should either.

If you broke down and ate three unnecessary donuts to medicate your broken heart, God would NOT say, "Suzie, you are a BAD person! Now, I'm going to turn my back on you and not let you into heaven!" He would say, "Suzie, sweet child, what's wrong? Are you sad? What was it that led you to try to find solace in donuts? Come to me and I will heal you."

If you aren't sure he'd say the latter, or if his mercy and grace are new concepts for you, you definitely need to finish this book and continue to read about the subject of "grace."

Anytime you read a purportedly Christian diet book, filter the information you read about how to eat through what you know about God. Does the message bring forth the fruit of the Spirit? Does it center on love and peace and joy and relationship, or does it engender fear, unfounded guilt, shame, and depression? If the message condemns you, then know it's not God who has been whispering in your ear.

How This Book Is Laid Out

The Eden Diet is organized into three main sections. In part 1, "A New Paradigm for Weight Loss," I help you spot the lies you've been fed regarding food and eating. You can't see how the truth fits together until the false ideas have been removed. I challenge the notion that you have to restrict normal food from your diet when you're trying to lose weight. I show you how the diet mentality actually makes you fat. And I show that eating fattening treats in small amounts and with intention can actually help you lose weight.

In part 2, "The Eden Diet: How to Get Skinny Eating Normal Food," I explain God's plan for eating and how following it will naturally lead you to your ideal weight. I show you how to tune in to your hunger pangs and how to feed them the way God intended, with a proper attitude and with a proper amount of food. And I show you how to eat (or not eat) as an act of worship.

In part 3, "How to Beat Temptation," I reveal how to overcome the temptations that cause you to eat in the wrong ways. I help you identify when emotions, sin, bad habits, and erroneous beliefs trigger you to eat for the wrong reasons. I also provide strategies to beat those temptations.

Finally, in the workbook, which is available separately on my website, www.TheEdenDiet.com, and through online and traditional bookstores, I provide even more tools that help you put the Eden Diet into action.

And God Said It Was Good

Now our journey together begins.

Let me describe to you the joy you're about to experience. If you read this book and adopt the Eden Diet for yourself, you will be freed from bondage. You're going to feel like a thousand-pound monkey has been lifted off of your back. You're going to be happier. You're going to be slimmer. And you're going to be healthier.

You're going to think about food as Adam and Eve did in the beginning: not often, and only when you're hungry. You're going to walk around less focused on food and more focused on God, to the point you actually forget to eat until your hunger pangs remind you.

Imagine. When you're hungry, you'll be able to eat even fattening, luxurious food, and you'll enjoy it a hundred times more—so much that you won't even want to eat the full serving. Half the food will bring you ten times the joy.

Not only will you be slimmer and more physically attractive, but also your joy will magnify your beauty. Everybody around you will want what you have.

Just think—you'll be a walking advertisement for the healing power of God.

Part One

A New Paradigm for Weight Loss

1

Overview of the Eden Diet

*Probably nothing in the world arouses more false hopes
than the first four hours of a diet.*

Dan Bennett

When I instruct male patients for weight loss, all I have to say is, "I want you to wait until you feel hunger pangs before you eat, and eat what you like but eat less, okay?" Then they respond, "Oh ... Okay, Doc!" and return three months later, weighing twenty pounds less. Just like that.

Women are more complex. Given the same instructions, they fight back, saying, "BUT ... I thought you were supposed to eat breakfast as soon as you open your eyes in the morning!" "BUT, I thought you were supposed to eat ten small, scheduled meals." "BUT, I can't eat bread because of the carbohydrates!" But! But! But!

Yes, I'm saying that, at the end of three months, my male patients return thinner, whereas a larger proportion of my female patients still have their big "BUTS."

Nearly everyone knows that men have the physical advantage when it comes to weight control. Their bodies are designed so that they lose weight more quickly. However, in terms of weight control, men also have the psychological advantage. Their minds are less cluttered with bogus dieting rules and regulations that cause women to think themselves into a hole. They're not bogged down with all those "have to" and "can't do" beliefs about weight control that make women crazy —and overweight.

In terms of weight control, my male patients tend to be like the "new wineskins" that Jesus referred to in the parable of the wineskins. They're more accepting of fresh, new contents when I give them advice. In the parable of the wineskins, Jesus said,

> No one sews a patch of unshrunk cloth on an old garment, for the patch will pull away from the garment, making the tear worse. Neither do people pour new wine into old wineskins. If they do, the skins will burst; the wine will run out, and the wineskins will be ruined. No, they pour new wine into new wineskins, and both are preserved.
>
> MATTHEW 9:16–17

In that parable, Jesus was signaling to his listeners that the old ways of Jewish legalism and rule keeping were gone, and he was ushering in a new era of grace and mercy.

To apply this wineskin concept to dieting, I'm asking you to let go of your old ways of thinking. Instead, be flexible and accept new teaching, even if it requires you to let go of your old beliefs. If you're a chronic dieter, you need to relax your legalistic thinking and become more flexible, like a new wineskin. You must prayerfully seek the truth about how to lose weight in line with the instructions God programmed into your body, even if it conflicts with your old beliefs. It only makes sense to do that. If that rigid, old-wineskin diet mentality had worked for you in the past, you wouldn't be reading this book.

In this chapter, I explain why this book is different from the majority of other diet books out there, and then I introduce you to how you can best utilize this book for your benefit. That way you can reinforce and apply the Eden Diet principles more effectively and experience the fruit of the Spirit that God intended for you to have.

Conventional Wisdom
Is Not Always Wise

By now, you've probably heard conflicting advice about how to lose weight. One source might tell you to eat a big breakfast and a tiny dinner, while another might say you should eat ten small meals in a day to jump-start your metabolism.

Or perhaps you've heard that you should cut out carbohydrates and eat only protein and fat so you can go into the fat-burning mode known as ketosis. Or that you should eat only high-fiber and low-fat or nonfat. Or that to lose weight quickly, you must eat only grapefruits, honey, and vinegar for three weeks straight.

In fact, you've probably been bombarded with so much information (and misinformation) about weight loss that you're entirely confused about what you should do. Or worse, because you followed diets destined to fail, you became not only confused, but you also gained even more weight and became depressed.

Trust me: it can be bad to have too much information about weight control. Having weight-control "knowledge" gives you a false sense that you can manipulate the metabolism God created. But you can't. No matter what biochemistry or physiology tricks you learn, you can't outsmart the weight-control system God created—not for long, anyway.

Consider the popular notion that you should have numerous small meals instead of three larger ones. On the surface, it sounds reasonable—even desirable. Who wouldn't want to eat ten times a day?

However, what if we were talking about a different bodily function, like urinating? I doubt you would ever say, "From now on, I'm going to urinate ten times a day because I heard it was good for me." Rather, you would trust your internal signals and wait until your bladder gave you the urge. You would let your normal, God-given programming flow automatically and naturally, without overthinking or trying to override the process.

Try to do the same with hunger. Forget about food in between meals, and trust your hunger pangs to remind you to eat—just like God intended when he gave you those hunger pangs. If you eat frequent small meals, let it be in response to your hunger pangs, not because your conscience is trying to follow some kind of man-made schedule.

Forget About What the World Says — Look at What God Says

I call this book *The Eden Diet* for a very simple reason. If we became obese by eating and thinking in ways contrary to how God intended, we can heal our obesity by returning to his original plan—the way it was in Eden.

Don't take the name too literally, though. I'm not saying we should live in the forest and forage for nuts and berries. And I don't think we need to eat only vegetarian, organic, all-natural, homegrown food.

On the contrary: I'm a city girl. I like air conditioning in the summer and a heated home in the winter. I like my pillow-top king-size mattress, and I enjoy eating processed foods and grilled animal flesh as much as the next gal.

I am only suggesting that we try to reclaim a *part* of how it was in Eden. Those of us with weight-control problems must try to tune out our heads and tune back into our bodies' internal signals for the weight-control guidance. We must forget the potentially harmful rules the world gives us about what, how, and why to eat, and rely on the brilliant internal weight-control program God gave us in the beginning: hunger pangs. And we must move around more as we work and play.

When we do those things, we can eat delicious, fattening foods forbidden from traditional reducing diets and still lose weight.

It's simple, right? Doesn't it sound natural? I'll teach you how to do it in this book, and soon you'll be losing weight the easy, natural way, in line with God's original plan, and without dieting.

I Can Eat *What*?

You can stop rubbing your eyes in disbelief now. You read it correctly. I am a certified medical doctor with an Ivy League nutrition background and obesity research experience, and I said it's okay to eat fattening food as you lose weight.

If you want to, you can eat meat-lover's pizza, ice cream, chocolate, or whatever else you like. You can eat processed and fast foods if you want to. Rejoice! The only limiter is that you have to eat those foods in smaller amounts than the world would have you believe is normal, and you have to wait to eat until you actually feel hunger pangs.

When my brother-in-law first read my book, he said I should have called it *The Eatin' Diet*. Maybe he's right. On this plan, even though you're eating smaller portions, you feel like you're eating a ton of food, and you feel incredibly satisfied. That happens because you let go of your guilt and actually pay attention to and enjoy each morsel that you put in your mouth.

Does this weight-loss philosophy surprise you? With a title like *The Eden Diet*, you probably expected me to tell you to eat food you might have found in Eden—food that is green, leafy, or grows on trees. Or maybe you expected me to advocate an organic or low-fat, no-sugar diet. But that's not what I'm saying at all. This plan is not about what food is right or wrong to eat.

God is merciful. He knows your weaknesses, and he knows what it will take to help you lose weight. Besides, he never said it was wrong to eat fattening food—not even for people who are overweight.

Disclaimer

You should check with your doctor before starting this plan. There may be foods you should not eat or exercises you should not perform for medical reasons. You may be allergic to certain foods, you may be on medicine that interacts with food (like some blood thinners and depression medicines), or you may have medical conditions that require a specialized diet (heart disease, diabetes, high blood pressure, kidney disease, etc.).

In those cases, you might consider asking your doctor about how much in the way of treats you're allowed. Ask him or her if it's okay to cheat on your medical diet to help you stick to a weight-loss program long term. After all, the benefits from your weight loss may more than overshadow any negative consequences from a temporary departure from your ideal diet.

Don't worry; if you are not allowed to deviate from your ideal diet, you can still benefit from this plan. You can learn how to avoid eating for the wrong reasons, and you can adopt a healthier attitude about food and exercise.

The Seven-Day Challenge (As Though It's a Challenge!)

Your first commitment to this plan need be for only seven days. The number seven is significant. In the Bible, it appears numerous times and is considered to be the number of completion.

What am I asking you to complete in your first week? Your main assignment will be to finish reading *The Eden Diet* in its entirety. Whether or not you complete it will be a litmus test. Are you really as committed to losing weight as you say you are? Some people just want to think and read about losing weight without actually doing it. They read diet books for entertainment. I suppose it makes them feel less guilty—as though they're actually doing something productive to rectify their problem.

But the truth is you must accompany thinking with positive action if you want to succeed. The apostle James wrote, "Faith without deeds is useless" (James 2:20).

Are you ready to accompany your faith with deeds? Are you ready to join with me wholeheartedly? It's time to decide.

Don't worry; if you go with me, it will be easy. It will be so easy, in fact, that you won't want to stop. You will lose weight so effortlessly and feel so joyous that you will wonder how on earth you ever made it through the first week on other diets.

The Seven-Day Challenge

1. Read through *The Eden Diet*.

2. Wait until you feel actual hunger pangs before you eat.

3. Eat small portions of normal food — just barely enough to take away your hunger.

4. When you are tempted to eat when you're not hungry, turn to God and pray.

During the first week, your main assignment (besides reading the book) is to wait until you feel actual hunger pangs — when your stomach is completely empty — before you eat. You also have to eat small portions of normal food, whether it's grilled chicken or french fries or chocolate cake. Eat what you like, but just barely enough to take away your hunger — perhaps a third to half a normal portion, and only when you're actually hungry. That's it.

To beat the temptation to eat when you're *not* hungry, turn to God and pray. Or become distracted in some other healthy activity.

Remember that as soon as you feel the next wave of bona fide hunger pangs, you can eat a little bit of that exact food that tempted you earlier when you weren't hungry. You're not really denying yourself; you're just delaying gratification until later.

Easy, right?

The Thirty-Day Measure of Success

On this plan, you will measure your progress in thirty-day blocks, using a chart that you may photocopy and fill out. You might ask, "Why thirty-day blocks?" The answer is simple. Thirty days is a convenient amount of time in which to measure your progress. It's long enough to experience a change in attitudes and in your weight, but it's not so long as to be tedious. It's an amount of time many people are willing to commit to for a trial run. And we're used to measuring time in months. That's it. There's no magic or heavy-duty science in that number.

That's why there are so many thirty-day money-back guarantees. We are willing to try new things for thirty days. By the end of that time, we usually decide we like the product and want to keep it. I believe that's what you will do in this case if you just give the program a chance.

So after you've finished the Seven-Day Challenge, spend some time filling out your Thirty-Day Record, using the chart. For example, you may set a goal such as "This month I will focus on always leaving a little food on my plate," or "This month I will focus on how my body feels when I eat healthy food versus junk food."

When you set your thirty-day goals, do it prayerfully. The mistake you may have made in the past was to leave God out of the equation. You really don't have control over your destiny, do you? Of course you don't. So don't determine what will happen in the thirty-day blocks based on your personal willpower. Ask God what he thinks you need to work on and go from there. And then write, "God willing, in the next thirty days, I will . . ."

It only makes sense to do it that way. God knows more about what we need than we do. Each of us has a unique set of circumstances that contributed to our food issues, and each of us is affected to a different degree physically, emotionally, and spiritually by our weight problems. So we need prayerful, individualized plans for our thirty-day blocks.

Another benefit of setting individualized behavioral goals is that it allows you to compare yourself to yourself rather than compare yourself to others. Other people may need to focus on different behaviors than you do.

Remember, comparing yourself to others sets you up for failure. On the one hand, if you compare yourself to those who don't lose as

My Thirty-Day Record

Block # _____

Start Date _____   End Date _____

Starting Weight _____   Ending Weight _____

Starting Measurements   **Ending Measurements**

Chest _____   Chest_____

Waist _____   Waist_____

Hips _____   Hips _____

Thighs _____   Thighs _____

Arms _____   Arms _____

Behavioral Goals

This month, I will focus on:

1. _____

2. _____

My experience with those behaviors:

_____

_____

_____

_____

_____

_____

much, you may become prideful, and you know what the Bible says about that. On the other hand, if you compare yourself to those who lose more weight, you might feel inadequate and become depressed.

It's okay to weigh yourself at the end of the thirty-day blocks of time, but I ask that you don't set particular weight-loss goals to achieve. Instead, *set one or two behavioral goals, and let the pounds fall where they may.* When you do that, you will feel less pressure, and that's always a good thing.

In subsequent months, you may add additional behavioral goals to your list if you believe it's necessary, but do so prayerfully. One mistake that people make is expecting too much from themselves too fast. Remember, Rome wasn't built in a day.

Over the Hump After Thirty Days?

I would love to tell you that you'll be home free and invincible after thirty days, but it doesn't work that way. Current neurobiology literature absolutely supports that changing habits changes nerve pathways in the brain. However, it does not come close to suggesting a specific time frame for how long it takes to change habits. Nor does it suggest how long those brain chemistry changes stick if you revert back to your old habits.

Clearly, neurons (nerve cells) are known to have plasticity, which means they are moldable to an extent. In other words, your brain will soon forget what you taught it if you don't keep up the good behavior.

This modern information is, unfortunately, contrary to the popularized notion that it takes twenty-one days of repetition to ingrain a new habit. That notion originated back in 1960 with a book called *Psycho-Cybernetics*.[1] Unfortunately, the author of that book, Dr. Maxwell Maltz, based his theory on anecdotal observations as a plastic surgeon and on a paucity of research. The theory is clearly outdated in modern scientific circles, but it is a myth that hangs on tenaciously in the lay community. Innumerable authors have cited this notion as though it were an accepted, proven fact.

The take-home message is if a diet program promises you a quick fix or a permanent change for your bad habits after twenty-one (or thirty) days, it's just telling you what you want to hear. The fact is we're forever in a state of flux. We can either reinforce or work against our newly adopted attitudes, depending on the choices we make in the present. Put another way, you can fall off the wagon at any time, no matter whether or not you think you made it "over the hump" by making it to the thirty-day mark.

In this microwave society, we want everything fast and easy, and that includes changes in our habits and attitudes. But God knows it doesn't work that way. That's why Paul said in Romans 12:2 that you can "be transformed," with the implication that it will be a continual transformation as long as you live.

But here is the good news: psychologists say that the more you act a certain way, the more your attitudes will begin to agree with your actions, and the easier it will be to continue to act that way. In other words, your actions affect your attitudes and your attitudes affect your actions. The two reinforce each other. That's probably why the longer you stay on this plan, the more natural it feels to say no to unnecessary food and eat according to your bodily signals.

Don't just take my word for it, though. Trust your own experience. How do you feel now that you're on the seven-day challenge? Don't you feel great? Don't you feel liberated? Aren't you excited? Then of course you can make it through the first thirty-day block. And you can make it through all the other thirty-day blocks too.

There really is no getting over a hump on the Eden Diet. Your old diet mentality was the hump. Now it's all downhill—easier. Being on this plan for thirty-day blocks will be more like coasting than climbing. It is true that you will face challenges on this plan, just as you face challenges on any plan. But you can have victory over them. This time you're doing it with God on your side—and in manageable thirty-day increments.

Phases of Change

Even though I don't hold you to meeting deadlines during your thirty-day blocks, you will probably find that you naturally go through phases anyway.

Initially, most people revel in the joy and liberation of being able to guiltlessly eat food they enjoy again. It's like being released from prison. You think, "Woo-hoo! I'm free!" Maybe you'll even eat ice cream for breakfast, lunch, and dinner for a couple days.

I promise ... that party phase won't last very long. If it does, you will only end up feeling sluggish, tired, and generally gross. Fantastic! It will teach you a lesson. Soon enough, you'll learn to prefer the healthy food that makes you feel better physically. At least, you'll prefer healthy food most of the time.

In time and through trial and error, most people settle down with a diet that consists of a nice balance of the healthy food that nourishes them and the decadent treats that make them feel satisfied emotionally. When they eat junk, they learn to eat it in smaller amounts—a few bites of dessert at the end of a small, otherwise healthy meal, for example. That's why they can continue to lose weight.

No matter how slowly or quickly you progress on this plan, and no matter how many times you backslide, you'll still be better off in the long run than you would be with traditional dieting. You already know from firsthand experience that traditional diets don't work for long-term weight control.

Now that you have an overview of the diet, let's get busy exposing the lies and replacing them with the truth about how to lose weight.

2

Say Good-Bye
to the Diet Mentality

*To promise not to do a thing is the surest way in the world
to make a body want to go and do that very thing.*

Mark Twain, *The Adventures of Tom Sawyer*

I offered every treatment I knew to my young patient with neck and
shoulder pain, but nothing helped her. Finally, I ordered MRIs of her
painful areas to see if I was missing something. When the scans came
back totally normal, I began to consider that perhaps her pain was
more emotional than physical.

As I examined her neck again, I asked her, "Is something going on
in your life that's a pain in the neck? Are you shouldering some sort
of burden? Is it school? The family? The boyfriend?"

I was amazed by what transpired next. As soon as I said the word
"boyfriend," her neck muscles tensed up under my hand. That's when
she first began to open up about the abuse.

This girl was both smart and pretty, but she was going out with a
real jerk of a boyfriend. He told her she was fat, ugly, and stupid, and
that, if she left him, the next boyfriend would treat her even worse.

I suppose that's why she bought the first edition of my weight loss
book a while back. On some unconscious level, she must have figured
that if she could lose weight, she'd finally be good enough for her
Prince Charming.

My book was not what she expected. When she came back for her follow-up appointment, she had only read the introduction and then stopped. I guess my book scared her, in a way. She said, "If I stop dieting now, I'll gain *even more* weight and then nobody will want me—not even him. My weight problem is my own fault, anyway. I have no willpower."

The ironic thing is this girl was probably ten pounds overweight at most. Her real problem wasn't her weight. Low self-esteem and fear of the unknown kept this girl both on a chronic diet and in a bad relationship. Ironically, the chronic dieting, which was her emotional crutch, led to further weight gain and further entrenched her in the bad relationship. It was a vicious cycle.

How about you? Do low self-esteem and fear of weight gain keep you on a perpetual diet? And does the dieting, in turn, cause you to gain rather than lose weight over time? Causing you to go on yet another diet to repair the damage caused by the previous diet?

If the answer is yes, don't feel bad. A lot of people are just like you. Eighty percent of those who diet and lose weight regain it after one year.[1] But, they keep going back on diets because dieting is all they know.

It's heart-breaking. We pour our very souls (not to mention our money) into weight control. Each year, Americans spend over $50 billion to see doctors, take diet pills, join commercial weight-loss programs, buy expensive diet food, and undergo laparoscopic banding or gastric bypass weight-loss surgeries. And, despite all of our money, heartache, and effort, we grow heavier and heavier over time.

In this chapter I discuss the biology and psychology of why dieting doesn't work—how it preys on people with low self-esteem and how it messes up your metabolism and contributes to depression, anxiety, and eating disorders. I also look at dieting from a spiritual point of view. I discuss primarily New Testament Scripture and show how dieting causes us to violate four rules God gave us about how to eat.

Do We Have Split Personalities or What?

Why do we keep dieting when we fail at it so frequently? I once heard that the definition of insanity is repeatedly doing something that doesn't work but expecting a different outcome. Maybe we're all insane.

Okay, I don't really think we're insane because we diet, but it does seem kind of crazy to keep doing something that doesn't work. If our dieting habits don't seem to be working, then let's try to figure out why.

At first glance, dieting seems logical. If you suppress your hunger pangs and restrict the number of calories you take in, you should be able to lose weight. It's not rocket science. It's just hard, cold accounting: calories in versus calories out.

But, if we look closer, we find the root of the problem. We're not calculators; we're people. We're imperfect; we're fallen; and we have a hard time resisting the temptation to eat. In other words, even though the concept of dieting is logical, when you apply it in the context of real-life human imperfection and sin, it doesn't actually work.

The reason I think traditional diets don't work is that we humans have a combination of two opposing desires. We have a strong spiritual desire to love the Lord and to obey him by eating perfectly and caring for his temple. At the same time, we have a strong fleshly desire that compels us to love ourselves more than God and thus overeat.

As Paul said:

> So I find this law at work: Although I want to do good, evil is right there with me. For in my inner being I delight in God's law; but I see another law at work in me, waging war against the law of my mind and making me a prisoner of the law of sin at work within me.
>
> ROMANS 7:21–23

As far as I'm concerned, this is the problem: we want to do what's right, but, at the same time, we don't want to do what's right. We have two different desires fighting against each other in our minds. Maybe we *are* crazy.

Given our susceptibility to sin, which is the other law Paul saw working in his body, our dieting methods are destined to fail. So long as we're this conflicted—and we'll be this conflicted until we're in heaven—we simply won't be able to make the right and godly choice every time we eat.

What we need is a weight-loss program that takes our split personalities into account and allows us to succeed at weight loss anyway. That's what the Eden Diet is all about. It's the perfect method for imperfect people like me to achieve weight loss. I hope it will work for you, too. Not that you're imperfect or anything.

What Is and What Isn't a Diet?

A diet is simply the way a person eats in his or her normal daily routine. Everyone who eats is on a diet of some sort, whether it's an all-you-can-eat "see-food" diet that leads to weight gain, a healthier diet that's prescribed for medical reasons, or a diet that's somewhere in between.

That explains how I can be against traditional dieting but still use the word *diet* in my title. It's a matter of semantics. I'm not against all diets. I'm only against traditional weight-reduction dogma and legalism, mostly because those things usually cause us to gain weight in the long run.

With those semantics out of the way, let's look closer at what's wrong with traditional reducing diets.

Traditional diets normally require you to eat measured quantities of low-calorie food at set times and to deny your hunger pangs. They also forbid you to eat the fattening treats you tend to crave, like sweet desserts, breads, starches, and high-fat foods like cheese, butter, ice cream, and fried foods.

When you're on a traditional reducing diet, you think of it as being separate from regular life. You either go "on" a diet in your weight-loss routine, or you go "off" a diet and back into your usual, fattening routine. It's feast or famine.

Now let me define what a diet isn't. A diet isn't a means to address the question of why you became overweight to begin with. It doesn't rectify the underlying attitudes that led you to accumulate unwanted fat, and it doesn't probe into how your emotions, your past experiences, your rationalizations, and your sinful nature led you to gain weight by confounding your interpretation of hunger.

A diet certainly doesn't retrain you to eat normally, either. I don't know a single normal, slim, healthy eater who precisely measures quantities of preapproved foods and eats at predetermined times according to a written set of rules. This is distinctly abnormal.

For another thing, because dieting causes you to spend much of your time hungry and disallowed from eating, it makes you think more about food than ever. You obsess about when and what your next meal will be and worry that you might not be able to hang on and resist the hunger pangs until then.

A diet is a distinctly abnormal way of eating, yet you expect it to teach you to eat normally. You think you will emerge on the other end as a "normal" eater, and you will be able to keep the weight off permanently.

Why do you continue to think that way? It doesn't make sense!

Does God Say We Should Stop Dieting?

I wish I had a notarized statement from God on the subject: "Dear children, thou shalt not diet." Or, "If thou beest pudgy, thou can still partake of thy Baklava—but eateth less and eateth of it more slowly." However, God never specifically told us how to manage our weight. He told us only how we should eat.

That's right, he told us how we should eat. Let's look.

In the Bible we find four guidelines:

1. We shouldn't be gluttonous (Proverbs 23:2, 20–21).
2. We shouldn't worry about or think too much about what we will eat (Matthew 6:25).
3. We can eat any type of food (Mark 7:15–19).
4. We should eat to the glory of God (1 Corinthians 10:31).

Hear me now: *Dieting causes us to break all those rules.* First, diets encourage gluttony. When we are told we shouldn't eat ice cream, all we can think about is eating ice cream. Eventually, our dietary restraint breaks down, we lose control, and we finish off a whole quart so we can throw the container away and get rid of the temptation. If that's not gluttony, I don't know what is.

Second, diets cause us to worry about what we will or will not eat. Will we be able to find the right groceries at the store? What if someone eats our special food by mistake? Will we be able to eat the right amount of the right food at the right time? Will we be able to resist temptation? What happens if we have to go to a party or out to dinner?

And if we weren't worried about how we should eat before we went on the diet, the experience of deprivation itself will probably turn us into worriers thereafter.

Third, diets make us think we can't eat any kind of food we want. They make us feel we should eat diet food, when everybody else gets to eat normal food. Yet Jesus declared that all food was fit to eat when he said what comes out of us (our behavior) is more important than the food that goes into us (Mark 7:15–19). He didn't tell us that people who are overweight have to follow a different set of rules or eat special food.

Fourth, diets do not cause us to eat to the glory of God. When we diet, we eat to the glory of ourselves, because we do it to make ourselves more slim, sexy, attractive, and powerful.

It's almost as if some evil genius designed the concept of dieting with eerie precision so he could cause us to self-destruct. I don't have to tell you who the evil genius is. You already know.

Dieting Trends Change, but God Never Changes

When my pastor, Mark McAdow, was in seminary, one of his class-mates had to deliver a "mock" sermon to the class and then be cri-tiqued on his delivery. The guy got up, grabbed a seat cushion off of one of the big, throne-like chairs on the altar, held it up, twisted and turned it, punched it, and then put it on the floor and stomped on it with his feet. He did that for a solid minute, at least. Afterwards, he held it up over his head and said, "This pillow is like the Word of God. Some people twist it and others attack it. But, it never changes." That was the entire sermon. After that, the guy put the pillow back on the altar chair and sat down.

The truth of God never changes.

When I was in college, the prevailing weight loss trend was to cut out fat and eat high fiber. A few years later, the trend was to eat low carbohydrate and especially to cut out sugar. After that, it changed to eating big breakfasts and small dinners. And then, it shifted to eating multiple small meals instead of a few large ones.

Compare this with the advice in the eating-disorder literature, which has remained the same over the years. It has always advised us to become more responsive to our internal cues and eat more flexibly in response to hunger pangs.

If you ask me, the ever-changing nature of the dieting literature should be our first clue that diets don't work for long-term weight con-trol. As the young seminary student said, worldly ideas consistently change, but godly ideas never change.

God gave us hunger pangs in the beginning for an important rea-son: they are good for us. They are God's wisdom in telling us when to eat. And they are just as important today as when God first pro-grammed them into Adam and Eve.

If you want to succeed at weight control, trust your God-given hunger pangs rather than the ever-changing weight-control fads of the nutrition world.

Dieting Puts Us in Bondage

Once upon a time, when I was on the dieting and overeating roller coaster, I felt like I was in bondage to food. My first thought when I woke up in the morning was either, "Feed me!" or "I hope I don't eat too much today," depending on which part of the roller coaster I was on.

My thoughts were focused to an unhealthy degree on food and eating (or on not eating), and on recipes and such, to the point where I felt that food controlled me, rather than the other way around. I was its prisoner.

I was actually afraid of food. I loved it and hated it at the same time.

I worried about what I would eat. I feared that I could not maintain my weight loss. I felt guilty when I failed to control myself. And I reacted to emotions incorrectly by stuffing them with food.

I was afraid that if I relaxed my restraints and allowed myself to eat fattening food, I would not be able to stop eating. I thought I would devour food like a frenzied piranha because of the tension I felt from holding back my desire to eat.

However, when I read the compulsive eating books, I realized that the bondage existed only in my head. It wasn't true that I was supposed to be on a perpetual diet. It was a lie.

How did I get out of bondage? I learned to eat fattening food with intention and not like a piranha. By the grace of God, I learned how to eat it in small amounts and only when I was hungry. Consequently, I reestablished the correct pecking order in the hierarchy: Jesus is Lord over me, and I am the boss over the food. This is how I believe God meant it to be in the beginning.

If It's Forbidden, We Want It Even More

Have you ever wanted something even more because you were told you couldn't have it? Sometimes you didn't want the thing at all until you were told you couldn't have it. I should know. When I dieted, it was the story of my life.

The more I tried to restrain myself from eating the forbidden cupcake with fluffy white frosting and sprinkles, the more power the cupcake gained and the less control I felt I had over the cupcake. Finally, my restraint broke down, and I ate one. Then I figured, "I've already blown it, so I might as well eat the other five." You see, I had to eat all of the little devils so they would stop tormenting me.

The apostle Paul didn't write about lusting after forbidden cupcakes, but he did write about a similar concept. He said that simply because we have laws, our sinful nature can take hold of us and cause us to want to break those laws.

In Romans 7:8–9, he wrote:

> But sin, seizing the opportunity afforded by the commandment, produced in me every kind of coveting. For apart from the law, sin was dead. Once I was alive apart from the law; but when the commandment came, sin sprang to life and I died.

If we see a rule, it is human nature to want to break that rule. So take that idea and apply it to the laws of dieting, and we end up with the same problem. When we are told to avoid certain foods, we end up wanting them even more! The moment we're told, "You can't eat ice cream," all we can think about is ice cream.

That's exactly why regimented diets don't work for us 80 percent of the time. They attract us because we think having rules governing our eating will force us to make the right decisions. However, the rules themselves, because of our sinful nature, lead us to want to break them just because they're there.

Dieting Preoccupies Us with Food

This isn't just my analysis. It was proven in a landmark scientific study that was published in 1950 by Professor Ancel Keys and his colleagues at the University of Minnesota. In this study, 32 young, healthy, male military recruits who never before dieted were required to decrease their food intake by 50 percent for six months. The researchers then analyzed how the food deprivation affected the men psychologically.

If this sounds like a horrible study to participate in, I agree. However, the recruits got a few perks that made it seem worthwhile. By participating, they were excused from their military obligations.

Interestingly, during the period of decreased food intake, some of the men who were not particularly interested in food before the study began to show preoccupation with it. They studied cookbooks, collected recipes, and created weird food concoctions that they would likely have found distasteful previously. Some recruits smuggled food out of the dining area to eat it in private, and some hoarded not only food but also small cooking utensils.

Despite their lack of interest in food before the study, 40 percent of the recruits reported plans to engage in cooking after the experiment ended, and three men actually changed professions after the experiment and became professional chefs.

If that's not enough evidence that dieting makes you preoccupied with food, get this: some of these otherwise healthy, red-blooded young men reported that their thoughts about food exceeded their thoughts about women.

What's even more interesting is what happened during the three months after the food deprivation ended. During this time, the recruits were allowed to go back to eating as much as they wanted.

Interestingly, though none of the men reported binge-eating behavior before the study, a number of them engaged in uncontrollable binge-eating behavior after the food restriction ended—sometimes eating as much as 10,000 calories per day. They even reported beating themselves up emotionally and feeling guilty and ashamed about their lack of self-control.

Does any of this sound familiar?

Thankfully, by the fifth month of re-feeding, most of the men's behavior returned to normal. However, even as long as nine months after the deprivation ended, a subgroup of the men continued to report abnormal eating behavior and thoughts about food. There were no obvious factors that explained why some of the men experienced these long-lasting effects from the deprivation whereas others went back to normal.[2]

In case you missed the take-home message from this study, let me summarize it here: not only does prolonged food deprivation (a.k.a. dieting) make you preoccupied with food and eating; it leads you to binge-eat, as well!

Dieting Turns Us Into Restrained Eaters

In 1975, researchers coined a name for the interesting collection of behaviors that result from chronic dieting. They called it "restrained eating."[3]

Restrained eaters perpetually try to limit the quantity they eat and/or exert willpower to avoid certain foods they consider to be off-limits. But, at other times, when their self-imposed restraint breaks down, they over-eat. It's as though they cross an imaginary boundary line that separates "on a diet" from "off a diet." They think, "Well, I broke the rules of the diet. Therefore, I'm not on the diet anymore and I might as well go to town!"

Restrained eaters report excessive preoccupation with food, eating for emotional and other reasons, and sometimes binge-eating behavior.

Since the inception of the term "dietary restraint," researchers have exhaustively studied the phenomenon. For the sake of brevity, I will summarize the research in the remainder of this section, highlighting only the main points. Forgive me if I don't give credit to every researcher who contributed to this body of knowledge. The list would be too cumbersome.

The available research shows that observed breakdown of dietary restraint (losing control and overeating) is based on cognition (thinking). That's important because it shows that overeating can be a learned phenomenon. In other words, your stomach doesn't send out a chemical signal to make you break down and eat an entire pound of Oreos. It's your beliefs and attitudes about food and eating that make you do that. That's good news, because it means you can unlearn those beliefs too.

Virtually any stressor can lead to the breakdown of dietary restraint and therefore contribute to overeating. Proven stressors include the threat of failure at an assigned task (i.e. a threat to the dieter's self-esteem), the consumption of a prohibited food, the consumption of alcohol (which lowers your inhibitions), the sight or smell of food, the anticipation of deprivation later, and either hunger or anxiety.

Another stressor that causes restrained eaters to lose control is the belief that they've *already* overeaten. For example, when restrained eaters were forced to consume milkshakes prior to an ice cream taste-test, they ate about four times more ice cream in the subsequent taste-test than did the unrestrained non-dieter subjects.

Presumably, the more milkshake pre-load the restrained eaters consumed, the more they figured they had "blown it," and so they might as well finish the job by overeating the ice cream in the sub-sequent taste-test. As I said, they had an all-or-nothing attitude—if they'd already overeaten they might as well overeat more. That's the exact kind of attitude that leads to weight gain.

According to the research, restrained eaters tend to measure diet-ing intervals in terms of days. They have either good days or bad days, as judged by whether or not they overeat on that day. If they cross the diet boundary and overeat, they rationalize, "I blew it today, but tomorrow is a new day." So, they tend to continue overeating for the rest of the day, anticipating a fresh start (and deprivation) in the morn-ing. In so doing, they consume excessive numbers of calories and, hence, gain weight.

If you would like to read more about restrained eating, you can refer to an excellent review by Urbszat, Herman, and Polivy.

Now that I've bombarded you with a lot of technical information, let me rephrase what I said and turn it into actual advice. After all, you came to me for actual help and not for a psychology degree, right?

Basically, this is what you need to remember: if you're a chronic dieter and you've overeaten, don't wait until the next morning to start anew. Start over right away. Measure your success moment-by-moment, not in 24-hour blocks of time. If need be, catch yourself mid-donut and say, "Hey! Wait a minute! Why am I eating this? I'm not even hungry!" Then, cut your losses immediately. Wrap up the rest of the donut and eat it when you're actually hungry, without guilt and shame, and that donut will lose its magic grip on you.

Another take-home message is if you limit yourself to only "allowable" foods, and if you're constantly expending your mental energy to have a "good" day (stay within your diet boundaries), it won't take much to push you over the line. That's why I'm telling you to erase the line. When you truly believe you can eat any food, you're less likely to eat them with an all-or-nothing, feast-or-famine mentality.

Dieting Causes Anxiety

In hindsight, the first time in my life I felt real hunger was when I started to diet at age seventeen. Initially, I didn't feel anxious about being hungry. If anything, I felt exhilarated. It was almost as if I'd discovered something new and exciting. "Wow! I feel hungry! This is awesome! I must be losing weight!" I felt good about finally doing something to take care of my weight problem.

However, after a year of feeling hungry all the time, I changed my mind. I learned to hate hunger. It made me anxious. On some unconscious level, I wondered, "Will I have to live like this forever? Will I ever be normal? How long will I be able to stand these hunger pangs before I break down?"

I was so afraid of hunger that I even ate extra to avoid it. Sometimes, if I wasn't hungry at breakfast, I would eat anyway, just in case I might feel hungry later in the morning and have no food to eat. And I would eat extra at lunch if I knew I wouldn't have another chance to eat until dinnertime.

I'm not the only one who gets anxious on a diet. Do you remember

45

Dr. Keys' experiment on the military recruits? The recruits didn't just become more preoccupied with food; they also experienced increased anxiety, depression, mood swings, social isolation, and withdrawal due to the food deprivation.

At Cornell, I learned that even laboratory rats become anxious when you deprive them of food (as determined by watching the rats' behavior). When food becomes available again, they eat more than they did prior to being deprived. They also gain weight.

Maybe we're more like rats than we know. A study published in *Obesity Research* looked at changes in brain chemistry when rats were deprived of food and then refed sugar water. The rats' levels of certain pleasurable brain neurotransmitters changed, and they learned to consume excess sugar water after a period of starvation.[4]

Do you want to know my theory about why the rats might have preferred sugar water more after dieting than they did before? Sugar gets into the bloodstream very fast. It takes away hunger pangs much faster than starches, proteins, or fats. Voila! Sugar instantly medicates hunger-pang anxiety.

Maybe that's why I had a bigger sweet tooth after my diet ended than I did before it started. I learned that sugar gave me immediate relief from hunger-pang anxiety.

Thankfully, now that I'm a Christian, I view hunger differently than I once did. I'm not afraid of it anymore. God, who loves me, gave me hunger as a gift to help me.

Because I'm not anxious about hunger, I don't feel compelled to eat sweets to make my hunger go away instantly. Nor do I eat extra to prevent hunger. I just experience hunger for a while, thanking God for it, and then I eat. It's that simple.

Dieting May Contribute to Depression

Even if you diet successfully, it can be hard to keep the weight off. The most optimistic study I've found states that, "perhaps greater than 20% of overweight/obese persons are able to [intentionally lose greater than 10% of their body weight and keep it off for over one year]." In other words, the most optimistic study projects an 80 percent failure rate.[5]

How might this phenomenon contribute to depression? It has to do with a phenomenon that psychologists call "learned helplessness." If you repeatedly try to improve your situation but keep failing, you eventually give up hope, you stop trying, and you become depressed.

By my calculations, you can easily apply this concept to weight control. If you repeatedly fail at weight control, you may feel helpless to change your situation. You understandably lose hope. In turn, those feelings of helplessness and hopelessness may deepen your depression and further propagate the emotional-eating cycle.

I don't know about you, but if I had a tendency toward depression, I would not compound my problem by dieting in the traditional way. I would go easy on myself and employ weight-loss methods as forgiving and merciful as God is.

Dieting May Contribute to Eating Disorders

I first started losing weight in my junior year of high school. Initially, I ate only diet food because that's what conventional wisdom told me to do. I ate Lean Cuisines and apples and raw carrots and celery and steamed unbuttered vegetables.

Then, one day, I couldn't stand it anymore. I broke down and cheated. I scooped a little ice cream between two Chips Ahoy cookies and then hurriedly ate the concoction to get rid of the evidence. It was a 200-calorie misdemeanor, not enough to slow my weight loss, but it was just enough to make me feel like a failure.

Over time I graduated to committing full-blown felonies. By my fourth or fifth month of dieting, I was eating junk food nearly every day. I was still losing weight, but I felt out of control nonetheless.

I'm not saying that I was wrong to eat junk food while losing weight. And I no longer think of eating junk food as being a misdemeanor. Actually, I was quite right to have allowed myself daily reprieves from dieting. It's the only reason I was able to persevere on the diet long enough to lose seventy-five pounds.

It's just sad I *felt* like I was committing a crime when I ate that way. I didn't hurt anybody by eating a tiny bit of junk food. I continued to lose weight. So what was the problem? The problem was all in my head. I was too concerned with eating according to rules and regulations.

When I got to Cornell, I studied nutritional biochemistry. I rationalized that if I learned everything about how I should eat, it would somehow increase my willpower and I would be better able to stay away from junk food. Wrong.

As it turned out, knowing more about nutrition only made the problem worse. It led me to overthink how I should eat. I would think, "I had better eat that [fill in the blank], or I won't get all my nutrients for the day." You see, I didn't eat only the healthy food I thought I should eat. I also binged on the junk food I wanted to eat, especially when my dietary restraint broke down.

Couple that with the fact that the freshman meal plan was "all you can eat," and you can see I was doomed. In no time I gained fifteen pounds. The freshman fifteen.

Thankfully, by my sophomore year, I was led by the grace of God to the self-help section at the bookstore, where I was drawn to the books on eating disorders. As I perused those books, I finally realized that my erratic eating habits had a name. Because of my yearlong stint with dieting, I had become a compulsive eater. In a cyclical fashion, I would either binge or starve myself to make up for the binge. It was feast or famine.

I realized something else as I stood in the self-help section that day: the diet books and the eating-disorder books gave contradictory advice. The diet books advocated eating according to rigid external rules and regulations. In contrast, the eating-disorder books were all about eating more flexibly in response to your internal hunger pangs.

Talk about an "aha!" moment. Never in my whole life had I eaten in response to hunger. Either I stuffed myself as a child and never felt hunger, or I starved as a teenager so I could lose weight. In college, because starving and bingeing were all I knew, I vacillated between the two and became a compulsive eater.

Once I knew the reason for my strife, I also knew I had to give up dieting and start listening to my body's internal signals. Why? Because dieting, bingeing, starving, compulsive eating, anorexia, and bulimia are different faces of the same disease. All of them cause you to ignore your body's God-given hunger messages, which is never a good idea.

The Eden Diet May Help
Beat Eating Disorders

Back in that bookstore, I reasoned I had nothing to lose by giving up dieting. I already knew that the harder I worked at it, the more weight I gained. So I rejected the diet books and bought the books on compulsive eating.

The directions were pretty easy to follow. I had to remove the "have to" or "can't do" element from eating and apply a more natural set of questions to the eating experience. Do I feel physically hungry? Do I even like this food? Maybe I'm not hungry now, after all.

The recovery books recommended I broaden my idea of what food was allowable. I was supposed to eat not only healthy food, but also the more fattening foods I had previously thought were forbidden, like ice cream, pizza, bagels with cream cheese, and chocolate. The only restriction was that I was supposed to eat them in moderation and only when I was actually hungry.

As I got ready to start the plan, I admit I was a little worried. I thought I wouldn't be able to stop eating if I let go of my restraint. I thought I might go into a feeding frenzy and eat my way into oblivion. I was afraid I might get sick.

I was also afraid people would think I was a hypocrite. There I was studying nutrition at an Ivy League university, and I was about to allow myself to eat junk food intentionally. I felt like I would be committing nutritional blasphemy. I expected the nutrition police to come beating down my door at the mere thought of eating junk food on purpose.

But when I actually started the plan, nothing like that happened. I didn't eat my way into oblivion, and the junk-food police didn't arrest me. Instead, as I began to gain confidence that I could eat fattening treats whenever I wanted them, I found I didn't want them as much anymore. When I let go of my self-imposed bondage to those foods, I actually found freedom from them.

The surprises didn't stop there. When I experimented with eating previously forbidden foods like candy bars, but only when I was hungry, I found I didn't like the way they made me feel physically. I learned that eating too much of a very sweet food when you're hungry must be like taking the drug Antabuse if you're alcoholic. It makes you feel sick and therefore acts as a kind of negative reinforcement from eating too much the next time.

There I was, free to eat junk food but discovering that I felt sick when I ate too much of it. I learned to prefer healthy foods because they made me feel better. For the first time in my life, I craved healthy food. You can imagine my relief.

Do you want to know the best thing that happened when I gave up dieting? After a couple months of not dieting, I lost twenty pounds and had become thinner than I was before I went to college! In addition, I did it without feeling like I was doing something unnatural or forced.

Let me repeat—I gained weight while I was trying to diet and lost weight when I stopped dieting. Did you get that?

Dieting Feeds Our Desire to Control

Back in the days when I dieted, I remember feeling exhilarated in the first few days after I committed to do it. I believed I was finally in charge of my previously out-of-control weight problem, and I felt redeemed in my own mind because of it.

That in-charge, righteous feeling should have been my first clue that something was wrong. In reality, I don't have the power to redeem myself, do I? The last time I checked, God was the only one who could do that. Still, I am tempted by an unconscious desire for power to think I can do anything I want to do, including transforming my body by force of willpower alone.

However, when I dieted, my power high was short-lived. Most of the time, my willpower broke down when I couldn't stand the hunger pangs anymore. I let my cravings get the better of me, and I binged. After the binge, I felt powerless, guilty, remorseful, and bloated.

Interestingly, even though my power high was short-lived and I crashed afterward, I kept going back to dieting time after time. Why? In part because the initial "rush" made me feel so much better about myself.

Dieting Warps Your Metabolism

When you alternate between dieting and overeating (the yo-yo syndrome), you tell your body that your food supply is unreliable. In response, your metabolism adjusts so that it stores fat more readily. Basically, your body prepares for a famine in order to keep you alive. You turn your body into a very efficient fat-holding machine.

Soon after starting a restrictive reducing diet, your thyroid hormone levels fall, and so does your basal metabolic rate (BMR, the minimum amount of energy your body expends each day to keep you alive). That's bad news, because when you have a low BMR, you gain weight very easily.

If you go off your diet and return to normal eating, you're actually *overeating*. Even though you're eating the exact same number of calories you ate before the diet, your body has adjusted to the famine levels, so almost anything is too much.

Let's say you could eat 2,000 calories a day without gaining weight before your diet. After your diet, because of your body's increased ability to store fat, you might be able to eat only 1,800 calories a day without gaining weight. It seems so unfair, doesn't it?

Don't worry. I have good news for you. If you want to increase your metabolic rate and reverse the damage you did in the past, I show you how to do it in later parts of this book. Just keep reading.

Commercial Weight-Loss Programs
Rarely Help Long Term

If you don't succeed on your own, you might go to plan B, which is to join a weight-loss organization. You hold on to the idea that going to meetings or having a big support network around you will help you stick to the plan. You hope that increased accountability will increase your willpower.

I understand the draw. It can be fun to be involved in a group with people who share your interest in food and dieting. Sometimes you make good friends in those groups. Or maybe you can get a group of your overweight friends together and join the system as a group, making it a social experience as well.

Unfortunately, the benefits from joining don't seem to last. A study published in the *International Journal of Obesity* explored the rate of weight regain among participants in the Weight Watchers program.

Only those who were successful at reaching their goal were included in the study. Five years after losing weight, the respondents reported regaining an average of 56.4 percent of the weight they lost. However, keep in mind that the study was only on people who *met* their goal. Those average members who dropped out or failed to reach their goal were excluded.[6]

All this makes me wonder about a few things. How much weight does the average member regain? What proportion of all members reach their goal? How many of the members not included in the study weighed more after five years than they had before the program? Since that data wasn't examined in the study, I guess we'll never know.

To its credit, the Weight Watchers program was reported to achieve slightly better outcomes than the Atkins Diet.[7] However, I'm not convinced. If, after five years, the top dieters regained 56 percent of the weight they lost, it doesn't bode well for the average Jane or Joe who joins a weight-loss organization.

Why the Poor Outcomes?

There are several reasons why I believe commercial weight-loss programs don't work well for long-term weight control. One is that they cannot give you freedom from bondage. So long as you have to count points or calories or fat grams, you are not free. If you have to keep score of your food, you are saying, "I can't control myself around food, and I must have these external restraints on me or I will not eat properly."

Even with the apparent flexibility of the Weight Watchers point system, you end up more obsessed with food. If you have to think about how many points you have used and how many you have left, then you can't forget about food like you are supposed to. Remember, Jesus told us to not worry about what we will eat.

Another popular weight-loss program, NutriSystem, sells prepackaged meals. The benefit of this program is that you don't have to meticulously plan out your meals because the food is premade. You don't have to weigh your portions or calculate the calories. However, the disadvantage is that eating prepackaged food does not prepare you to eat in real-life social situations.

When you go to a wedding reception and everyone else is eating at the buffet, will you hide out in the bathroom and eat your prepackaged regulation dinner while sitting on the toilet? Will you abstain from joining your friends at a restaurant because it requires you to deviate from your plan? When your diet ends, will you feel prepared to join the rest of the world again, or do you plan to eat prepackaged food for the rest of your life?

My point is if you don't learn to eat normally when you are on your diet, how on earth are you supposed to learn how to eat normally when you go off the diet?

And what if you don't like their food? I guess that's too bad. Plus, prepackaged meals are often more expensive than the raw materials you can get at the grocery store.

These commercial programs may be great for some people as long as they continue to go to the meetings, but what happens when they cut the cord and stop going to the meetings? If they joined with friends for accountability, who are they accountable to when their friends drop out?

Finally, if you really think about it, when you join a commercial weight-loss group, you join a bunch of people who all have the same problem you do. At the meetings, you congregate with them to talk about food and recipes and about *not* eating, and that further feeds your obsession for food and eating.

Just go to the website for any of the commercial programs, and I'll bet you will find pictures of food as well as diet recipes, and you will find lots of other resources to keep you thinking about food and eating and not eating and everything else you need to stay confused and obsessed at the same time.

If you want to lose weight, take my advice: don't join an organization full of people who have a weight problem and are obsessed with food. It's like trying to learn from prison inmates how to succeed in the outside world. Instead, join with people who want to glorify God rather than food. Join an Eden Diet support group, where recipe-sharing and focusing on food are discouraged. Hang around with thin people and copy their habits. If you want to join a group, take an exercise class or join a book club where food and eating are not the focus. Get your mind off of food, eating, and dieting.

Conclusion

By now, you can tell what I think about traditional diets. And you can probably understand why we fail to control our weight so often when we employ them. The reason is that our culture's method of weight loss makes no sense from a psychological, physiological, or spiritual point of view.

If anything, dieting causes us to overeat because we want what we think we shouldn't have even more; it causes us to fear being hungry, which also leads us to overeat; it causes our metabolism to become more efficient at fat storage; and it causes us to enter into bondage to food and break the only rules God gave us regarding how to eat.

3

There Is No Bad Food

*The only time to eat diet food
is while you're waiting for the steak to cook.*

Julia Child

Sometimes, as I roll my cart down the aisles of the grocery store, I can't help but feel incredibly blessed. I remember my college days when I was broke all the time and could barely afford to buy groceries. Back then I used to buy those skimpy little diet dinners that you find in the frozen food section. They were so skimpy that sometimes I'd have to eat two of them to feel full. Only I had no business buying even one because they were expensive, and I didn't have money to spare, being a student.

What's really ironic is that I could have eaten at a fraction of the cost if I ate a PB&J sandwich or grilled cheese. I probably would have been more satisfied, too. I just didn't realize it at the time because I was delusional. I thought that normal food was off limits to me because it would make me fat.

If I continue to think about how much money I wasted on diet food in college, I go from feeling blessed to feeling irritated. By the time you compound the interest on the student loan money I used to buy those Lean Cuisines, it amounts to a small fortune.

In this chapter I will show how it doesn't pay to eat diet food, not only for cost reasons, but for a myriad of other reasons as well. You see, diet food can be fattening as well as expensive. In the end I hope to convince you to eat normal food in the proper way so that you can lose weight and save money, too.

The Lie of "Diet Food"

In the previous chapter, I challenged conventional wisdom and showed you why diets don't work well for long-term weight control.

In this chapter I'm building on that by explaining how diet food can be fattening as well as expensive. You see, I believe there really is no such thing as diet food. All food has calories, after all. And all food can cause you to gain weight, depending on the manner in which you eat it.

If you think a food is low in calories, you might eat a double portion when you're not even hungry, and therefore gain weight. Conversely, you can eat a small portion of normal food (like a meat, vegetable, and starch dinner) or a tiny portion of fattening food (like cake) and lose weight. Which sounds more desirable to you?

The designation of a food as being diet is merely an illusion cast by the food and advertising industries. And it's cast for the sole purpose of turning a profit.

If you don't believe me, check your favorite low-fat product to see how many ounces are in the package. Compare it to the nondiet version of the same product. You'll probably find that you get a smaller package of diet food for the same price as regular food, or you get the same size package at a higher price. Does that seem fair to you? Shouldn't you pay *less* money if you get fewer calories?

Because worldly lies and propaganda encourage us to eat diet food, it's important to understand the biblical truth about what food we are supposed to eat.

The truth is God gave us all foods. Not just diet foods. He did it so that we might eat and enjoy them as well as be sustained by them (Mark 7:15–19). We just forgot how to eat the more calorie-dense foods in the proper way (in small amounts) and at the right time (when we're hungry).

What Am I Calling "Normal" Food?

All food is normal and acceptable for eating because that is what Jesus said in the gospel of Mark. In the coming pages, you will find many examples of how to eat this normal food in a way conducive to weight loss.

Watch out, though, because I'm going to encourage you to eat food you previously considered to be dangerous—like cheeseburgers, pizza, and cookies. I do this because we tend to have a mental block about eating those foods while trying to lose weight, whereas we don't have a mental block about eating salads and other foods we know to be healthy.

At this point, I don't see the need to encourage you to eat healthy food. You already know you are supposed to, and I hope you continue to prioritize these foods in your diet. What I want is for you to see that all foods are on the allowed list for you now, both the chicken breasts and the occasional cheeseburger.

If it helps you to see through to the real spirit of this book, go ahead and substitute the words *grilled chicken breast* or *dark green, leafy vegetables* in the examples I offer about eating normal food. The truth is I'm not really pro–junk food. I'm just anti–food bondage.

We Tend to Gain Weight
When We Eat "Diet" Food

Before I understood food labels, I believed diet food was safer for me to eat. I thought I did not have the ability to control the quantity I ate. I reasoned that if I was going to lose control and overeat anyway, it might as well be on diet food, which has fewer calories. It was my version of damage control.

But I was wrong. At the time, I ate more exactly because the food was diet. I ate extra and I ate when I wasn't hungry, which in turn caused me to gain weight.

I read the labels that said sugar-free and must have unconsciously assumed the food was calorie-free. Therefore, I ate it anytime I wanted it or craved it or just *saw* it, regardless of whether or not I felt actual hunger pangs. And when I ate diet food, I ate portions that were too large.

Is any of this sounding familiar?

Extensive research by Cornell marketing professor Dr. Brian Wansink verified what I suspected from my own personal experience. He found that we eat more calories when we think the food is low-fat.

In Dr. Wansink's article "The Reoccurring Curse of Low-Fat Labels," which he posted on his Amazon.com blog on May 25, 2007, he pointed out that subjects who believed their granola was low-fat unknowingly ate an extra 35 percent, equaling an additional 192 calories, when compared to the intake of those who knew their granola was regular. Similarly, if research subjects knew their chocolate was low-fat, they ate an extra 23 percent.

In other words, we may think we're being clever by eating diet food, as though we are getting away with something, but we're only fooling ourselves. We eat larger portions and more calories when we think a food is diet.

The truth is we are better off eating regular food when we're hungry and sticking with small portion sizes.

We Can Lose Weight
by Eating Small Portions of "Normal" Food

One time an obese back pain patient of mine volunteered his weight-loss philosophy. He said, "If it tastes good, spit it out!" I love him dearly, but I'm afraid I had to disagree with him on that point.

Many of us believe that we gain weight because we eat "bad" food. We blame the fast food, the cheesecake, the chocolate, the french fries, or whatever else we perceive to be our weakness. We think, "If only I would give up [fill in the blank], I would finally lose weight."

We assume we have to give up bad food and even normal food if we want to lose weight. But that thinking is wrong. While it is more tempting to overindulge in rich, delicious food, it's the *amount* we eat that matters.

Take these normal meals: chili and cornbread, spaghetti with salad, grilled meat with veggies and a baked potato, soups and sandwiches, tacos, or chicken and dumplings. You can lose weight eating any of those meals if you eat the food in small portions.

You see, it really is all about calories in and calories out. As long as you take in fewer calories than you expend, you can still lose weight. It doesn't matter if you get 400 calories from two tomatoes stuffed with nonfat tuna or 400 calories from a half portion of a pot roast dinner. Those 400 calories are inside you no matter where they came from. You could eventually gain weight by eating 500 calories of salad and lose weight eating 400 calories of sloppy joe. When you eat fewer calories than what your body expends, you lose weight even if you're enjoying a juicy chili dog.

Doesn't this sound more fun than traditional diets? Isn't it great to know you don't have to prepare a special meal for you to eat while your family eats normal food? Isn't it great to know that you can go to any social event and eat what they serve? All you have to do is eat it in small portions and only if you're hungry.

I don't mean that you should eat *only* burgers and ice cream. Indeed, you shouldn't, even though those things can now be back on the menu for you. God gave you healthy food to eat too, and this is the food that truly nourishes your body.

We ought to eat the way French people eat, as my sister-in-law Missy wisely pointed out. Only about 7 percent of them are obese, compared with 31 percent of Americans. The French eat a varied diet. Not only do they eat rich, delicious, fattening treats, but they also eat salads, fruits, veggies, and other healthy food. They simply eat the rich food in very small portions, just as I advocate in the Eden Diet.

Let's Be Realistic — and Merciful

If you have lived in America very long, you've probably heard time and time again that there are certain foods you should eat to lose weight. You've heard that you must eat a diet low in fat; low in starches and sugars; high in fiber; and rich in lean proteins, fruits, and vegetables. In addition, we Christians know that our bodies are temples of God and that we should eat only healthy food to honor him.

The problem is, even though we know what we should do, we are clearly not able to do it. If anything, the more we try to live up to that puritanical ideal, the more weight we gain.

Speaking from experience, I understand the root of our problem. Our expectations are unrealistic. We expect obese people (the ones who have failed the most noticeably at weight control) to stay on the most restrictive reducing diets. It's crazy. Even thin people don't abstain from sweets or other junk food, nor do they eat according to a rigid schedule. So why do we expect the greatest sacrifice from those who can deliver the least?

I'm sure there are some exceptional dieters who have been able to succeed on restrictive reducing diets because they dieted as an offering to God. Because of their faith and pure intentions, I am sure they were empowered by him to succeed in spite of the deprivation. Their success is a wonderful testimony to God's transforming ability.

However, judging from the fact that I meet those exceptional people extremely rarely, and since such a small percentage of all dieters anywhere succeed at long-term weight control, I don't think that the ascetic approach is realistic for the vast majority. Most people I know who try restrictive diets are imperfect (like me) and tend to only be able to stick to them on a short-term basis.

In my case, when I strived to achieve a diet of nutritional perfection, my sinful desires took hold of me and urged me to binge. That's exactly why I learned to relax the rules and eat more junk food than dietitians typically condone.

When I stand before God, I hope he will say, "It's okay, Rita. I know you ate unhealthy food at times, maybe even too much, but in all, you lived longer because of your weight loss, and you used your problem to glorify me during those years. Good job! Now, about all those other things you did ..."

My point is this: God is all about mercy and love and not so much about adherence to legalistic codes of dietary law. I think he would be willing to look the other way if we occasionally violated the sanctity of our temple with junk food, especially when the end result is that we break out of bondage to food and enhance our relationship with him. Indeed, I think he would join us for burgers and fries and a thick chocolate milk shake—especially if it allowed him to minister to our other needs in the process.

Don't be fooled into thinking that God loves obedience for the sake of obedience. He doesn't love the Law for the sake of the Law itself, and he doesn't love nutrition rules and regulations for their own sake, either. Rather, he loves us, his children, the ones whom the rules and laws were designed to protect.

Won't You Get Sick if You Eat a Lot of Unhealthy Food?

Some people worry that they will develop malnutrition if they start eating more of what they want to eat and less of what they think they should eat. However, in all my years of practicing medicine, I have never seen anyone get sick due to a reducing diet.

Let's put this in the proper perspective.

You're right it could make you sick if you ate only junk food and never touched a salad or fruits and vegetables again. That's why Paul said, "'Everything is permissible for me'—but not everything is beneficial. 'Everything is permissible for me'—but I will not be mastered by anything" (1 Corinthians 6:12 NIV). I didn't say you should eat only junk food. In fact, I don't think you could do that for long, even if you tried.

Chances are that if you eat too much junk food, you will begin to crave healthy food fairly quickly. If you eat mostly sweets at one meal, at the next meal you will probably crave meat and vegetables. God's perfect design is at work, helping you to find a healthy balance.

You're also protected because many of your processed foods are vitamin fortified. In an industrialized country like the United States, you can't help but get some of your nutrients by accident. If you eat a bowl of vitamin-fortified, sugary breakfast cereal, you get a wider variety of nutrients than if you eat a bowl of broccoli. It's shocking but true.

I'll tell you the truth; we Americans worry about undernutrition needlessly in the vast majority of cases. Our more pressing problem is overnutrition. Not too many nutrients or vitamins—just too much food, period. Every single day in my office, I see eight or ten patients who suffer with diseases like high blood pressure, heart attacks, strokes, diabetes, cancer, worn-out knees and hips, and other illnesses caused, in large part, by the excessive intake of food.

However, don't just take my word for it. Find out from your own doctor if he or she is worried about you developing malnutrition if you eat a little junk on a reducing diet. If you're otherwise healthy, don't be surprised if your doctor tells you to take a multivitamin and not worry about it.

On the other hand, if you're ill with diabetes, high blood pressure, heart disease, cancer, or some other medical condition, it may be a different story altogether. You'll need to ask your doctor if you can safely eat treats without compromising your health.

Misleading Food Labels

In light of our tremendous exposure to advertising, we must become savvy to the media tactics that influence us. Otherwise we will not be able to filter out the misleading messages that lead to weight gain.

Let's consider the designations "fat-free," "sugar-free," "no added sugar," and "all natural." If a company calls a product fat-free, then the first thing you should do is read the label to find out how much sugar is in the product. Usually the manufacturer compensates for the removal of fat by adding extra sugar. Conversely, if it's called sugar-free or low-sugar, you'd better check the label for the number of grams of fat. Usually, if a product is low in one, it's high in the other. Otherwise the product won't taste good, and it won't sell.

I recently saw an advertisement for hard candy that claimed it was "fat-free," with the implication that it was therefore good for you. Well, of course it's fat-free—it's pure sugar. And guess what? Your body turns sugar into fat if you eat too much of it or if you eat it when you're not hungry. Suddenly, fat-free becomes fat-producing.

You also need to watch out for labeling that says "no added sugar." Not only should you check for the number of fat grams, but also check for the number of grams of simple carbohydrates (that's another name for natural sugar in this case). They don't have to add sugar if a product in its natural state is already loaded with sugar.

By the same token, if a product claims that it is "naturally sweetened," it doesn't necessarily mean it is low in sugar or in calories, nor is it necessarily more nutritious than its processed counterpart. It might contain honey, concentrated fruit juice, fruit puree, corn syrup, maple syrup, molasses, or sorghum, all of which increase the calorie content without adding much in the way of vitamins or minerals.

Just because a product is natural doesn't mean it's a good idea to eat it. Arsenic, cyanide, and hemlock are natural, and you wouldn't eat them, would you?

My point is you should be skeptical when you read labels that say "all natural," "fat-free," "low-sugar," "sugar-free," "no added sugar," or "naturally sweetened." They may lead some consumers to think the product is a freebie to overeat when it's actually not.

It's back to our previous statement: all food is fattening if you eat it when you're not hungry or when you eat too much of it. That's true even for low-sugar or natural food.

Misleading Serving Sizes

Buyer beware: watch out for misleading labeling on convenience-store–size packages of snack foods. If you look quickly or carelessly at the label, you might conclude that the entire bag of goodies is 250 calories. But if you read the fine print, you'll find that it's 250 calories *per serving* and there are *two* servings in the bag.

In other cases, a product's reported calorie count might be low, but it's only because the recommended serving size is very, very small. Currently, 100-calorie–size packs of muffins and cookies are being advertised for those who want to limit their portion sizes. In a way, I think it's great. It's definitely a move in the right direction to raise our awareness about portion size. Sometimes all you really need is a little taste of a dessert.

However, as an ex-compulsive eater, I would like to give you a word of caution. You have to think about eating 100-calorie packs with the right attitude, just as you should eat everything with the right attitude. If you eat a 100-calorie pack because you feel that you need to be rationed to 100 calories by an outside source or because you can't be trusted to stop eating the treat out of a regular-size package, then you're not truly liberated from bondage, are you?

In some cases, it might be better to forget about the 100-calorie micromuffins and rather choose to eat a quarter of or half an Otis Spunkmeyer giganto-muffin.

Did you notice that I said the word *choose?* Yes, I said you should choose to eat a portion of a larger muffin. You don't need some food company to police your eating. You can do it yourself. The reason is this: because of your association with Jesus, you are the lord over the food; the food is no longer lord over you.

Hidden Fats

Without fat, food loses that greasy-smooth texture that makes it so palatable. Thus, if a so-called diet food shows a low fat-gram count on the packaging but still tastes rich, then there is a reasonable chance that there is hidden fat in the product.

There are three types of fat that are commonly added to food: monoglycerides, diglycerides, and triglycerides. They share a similar chemical structure, and they all have 9 calories per gram. However, according to US government regulations, only the calories contributed by triglycerides have to be reported in the total calorie count of the product.

Mono- and diglycerides are not routinely counted in with the fat grams because they are usually added only in negligible amounts as emulsifiers. They keep the oil and water components from separating out into layers as the product sits on the shelf. But beware! Mono- and diglycerides can also be added in large quantities to supposedly fat-free products, thereby hiding a significant number of unreported calories in the product.

By law, a fat-free product is supposed to contain less than 0.5 grams of triglycerides per serving. However, there is no limit as to how many grams of mono- and diglycerides it can contain.

Let's look at the nutrition information reported for Promise fat-free margarine. The product is reported to have a calorie count of five calories per tablespoon. However, if you read the ingredients list, vegetable monoglycerides and diglycerides are the second item on the list, coming right after water.

If an ingredient is shown toward the beginning of the list, it means there is relatively more of that ingredient in the product. In this case, since mono- and diglycerides fall second on the list, it means that close to half of this so-called "fat-free" margarine could be hidden fat. In actual fact, its calorie count could be as high as 50 or 60 calories per tablespoon!

But we won't ever know the truth, because no company is obligated to report the calories from the mono- and diglycerides. Can you believe that's legal?

To avoid confusion or deception, the guidelines should be changed. Not only should triglycerides be counted toward the total number of fat grams, but so should mono- and diglycerides and all other types of fats with calories. I'm too busy to lobby for that right now, but if you send me a petition, I promise to sign it.

The take-home message is if you insist on reading food labels rather than listening for hunger pangs to guide your eating, then you really have to know what you're doing. If you eat low-fat food, learn to recognize the code words for hidden fat and pay attention to where those words fall on the ingredients list. If they fall high on the list, there may be a lot of hidden fat in the product. If they fall low on the list, then they may truly be present only in negligible amounts.

Better yet, stop relying on food labels to tell you how much of a product you can eat. It's too unreliable and too much trouble. Seriously, you have to have a PhD in chemistry to see through the marketing scams.

Here's an easier way: just rely on your stomach. Eat a small portion of whatever you like, and if you get hungry later, eat a bit more.

Diet Pie, My Foot

If you think a diet dessert is delicious, it's probably not as low in calories as you think. Consider all the diet pie recipes that are circulating. Most of them call for a tub of fat-free whipped topping (loaded with sugar), a package of light cream cheese (still high in fat), a low-fat graham cracker crust (still contains sugar), and sugar-free gelatin (the only ingredient that is legitimately calorie-free).

Maybe you assume the pie recipe is low calorie because it contains low-fat ingredients. Therefore, you have a second piece for taste, even though you aren't hungry for it. I should know; I used to do that all the time before I knew better.

If you do the math, you'll be disappointed. Add up all the calories in the ingredients and then divide by the number of pieces in the pie. When you do, you find that each piece of low-fat pie contains about 250 calories. That's as many calories as are in a regular-size candy bar. Since you had two pieces, you ate 500 calories' worth of diet pie. What was "diet" about it?

The fact is you could have eaten half a piece of the full-fat and full-sugar (and better-tasting) version when you were actually hungry, and it would have equaled only 150 calories. The half piece of regular pie might even have satisfied you more.

Even better, for a lot less money and effort, you could've eaten half a candy bar at 130 calories. You'd pay only 30 cents, and you wouldn't have to clean up dirty dishes, either.

Here's another example of a ridiculous diet dessert recipe. Have you heard of the low-fat cake recipe that calls for a box cake mix and a can of Diet Coke? The soda replaces the eggs and oil that you would normally add to the mix.

Here's the problem: the dry mix still contains flour and sugar, which means the cake still has calories, and it can still be fattening if you eat it when you're not hungry. As much as I wish it were true, Diet Coke does not actually erase the calories in flour and sugar when you consume them in the same sitting.

If you really want to go over the top, go ahead and slap some low-fat frosting on that cake and eat a double serving when you're not even hungry. Then go to your doctor and ask to have your thyroid checked because you don't know why you're gaining weight.

My point is: just because the recipe is called "diet" or has one or two ingredients in it that are sugar-free or low-fat, it doesn't mean it's a freebie or that you can eat it when you're not hungry. All food, even that which is labeled "diet," is potentially fattening when consumed improperly.

Diet Salad, My Foot

On those occasions when your family gets fast food, you might be tempted to order the salad instead of getting burgers like everyone else. Why? Perhaps you feel morally obligated to eat diet food because you are overweight. Perhaps you want to feel like you've allowed the family to get what they want, but you've managed to stay "good" for your meal.

But if your salad comes with cheese, high-fat salad dressing, croutons, dried fruits, bacon bits, or other calorie-dense toppings, then you might be eating more calories than are in a deluxe cheeseburger! What's worse, if you perceive that you have been deprived because you didn't eat the burger you really wanted, you might be tempted to eat something else after you get home, which would make your total calorie count even higher.

So you have to be sure the so-called diet food you're eating doesn't actually have more calories than you think. But you also have to remember that you may get less satisfaction from eating that food and will thus be tempted to repay yourself with more food later, even if you're not hungry.

You might be better off and more satisfied eating a half portion of regular food when you are hungry. That way you will probably save money too. Your double portion of diet food often costs four times as much as a half serving of regular food.

Be careful to understand the true spirit of my message. I'm not saying it's better to eat cheeseburgers rather than salad. It's actually very good to eat salad—provided the salad is largely vegetables. I, for one, actually prefer salad about half of the time. I am only saying that what you think is low calorie may not actually be low calorie. You should think of diet food the same as you think of any food. It is meant to be eaten only in small portions and only when you are hungry.

Diet Drinks Might Be Fattening

Once upon a time, I carried a can of Diet Coke with me wherever I went. I mindlessly and automatically took sips from it whether or not I was thirsty.

One day, out of the blue, I felt God speak to me as clearly as I have ever heard him. I believed that he was trying to tell me I should give up my Diet Coke habit—as in forever. It was as though I were a baby and my can of pop had become my pacifier. I would suck on it for comfort and security, just as a tiny little baby sucks on its bottle for comfort. I was actually in bondage to a can of soda. Can you believe it?

You could probably hear my piercing scream all the way to Kansas. "Oh, God ... please ... *no*! Anything but that! Take my right arm instead! I'll even give up chocolate if you let me keep my Diet Coke!"

I wasn't exactly sure if it was God or my better judgment speaking to me that day, but either way I decided I had better listen. I figured the voice must have known something I didn't know. So I went cold turkey on Diet Coke and haven't touched it in years.

In hindsight I know why I had to listen to that little voice in my head. When I drank pop without paying attention, it also caused me to put food in my mouth without paying attention. It reinforced my mindless, fattening, hand-to-mouth behavior. You could say that my Diet Coke–clutching hand had developed a mind of its own and was making me fat.

As if that weren't bad enough, by drinking diet pop, I had raised the threshold on my taste buds. Because they were constantly exposed to the sweet taste of the drink, they learned to expect sweetness all the time. For them to be impressed that a food was sweet, it had to be really sweet. When they didn't get more and more sweetness, they felt ripped off. If I drank plain water, they complained that it was bland, those spoiled little taste-bud brats.

Diet drinks also confused my body's self-regulating mechanisms. I was designed by God to feel satisfaction and relief of hunger after consuming sweet substances, but if I drank diet pop when I was hungry, after drinking it I still felt hungry. I disconnected the sweet taste stimulus from the normal response: the feeling of fullness. Then, when I ate real sugar, I didn't know when to stop eating it, and I ate too much.

I'm trying to say that I think drinking diet drinks may cause you to overeat sweet desserts because they confuse your body's response to sweetness. I don't know if it's true; it's just one of my many hypotheses.

I suppose that raises the question, "Which came first, the chicken or the egg?" Do diet drinks make you fat, or are you more likely to drink them because you are already fat? I think the answer is both. Obese people feel morally obligated to drink diet soda rather than regular soda because they want to lose weight, but then drinking diet soda compounds their weight problem.

In case you have any doubt, I am not encouraging you to drink regular pop instead of diet pop. The data shows that sweet pop is even worse for you, and its intake is consistently associated with obesity.

I'll tell you what I am encouraging you to do: lower your taste bud threshold back to normal by drinking water instead of sweet diet drinks. Then your dessert will taste sweeter and more special. You will also learn to reassociate consuming sweets with feeling satisfied, and you will break the habit of mindlessly and automatically putting unnecessary substances into your mouth.

Take note: I'm not saying you should replace one pacifier for another. Don't use your water bottle as a replacement pacifier for the can of pop. If you do, you'll just continue to reinforce the mindless hand-to-mouth behavior that makes you fat.

Instead, drink water when you're thirsty, just like God intended, and take sips of water in between bites when you eat to aid digestion and enhance your eating joy. You ought to get plenty of water that way.

Beware of Neon Liquids

To help you appreciate water again, I would like to point out how the advertising world may have corrupted your opinions about it. The advertisers want you to believe that water is bland, because there's big money in the beverage industry. If you think that your beverages must be flavored, sweet, or brightly colored to be interesting, then you'll spend $1.50 on the neon-colored sports drink at the vending machine after your workout. They want you to forget about the water fountain that replenishes your fluids for free.

The marketing hook is that those neon-colored sports drinks contain electrolytes. But do you really think you exercise to the same level of intensity as the Tour de France bicyclists or Olympic swimmers they show on TV? Probably not.

But if you do, I'll tell you a secret that will save you money. It's called the World Health Organization's oral rehydration formula. It's how to replace fluids and food energy the inexpensive way when persons in third-world countries become dehydrated. All you have to do is consume water plus a tiny bit of sugar and salt at the same time. The salt contains the electrolyte sodium. To get potassium, eat a banana or an apple the next time you're hungry. Or drink some diluted orange juice (for sugar and water) and eat a handful of pretzels (for sodium). Voila! I saved you a dollar.

I'm not saying you have to give up sweet and neon-colored drinks entirely. God gave you all drinks to enjoy—even the blue ones. I'm only saying you have to learn how to consume your sweet drinks in the proper way. You have to slow down and sip your sweet drink for taste rather than chug it out of habit for thirst. Sip it to the glory of God with respect and appreciation for his temple, your body.

Treat your sugary drink the same way you treat food, especially if it has calories. If you had a nice juicy steak, you wouldn't gobble it up in one mouthful, swallowing it whole like a dog, without even tasting it. You would realize how special it is, and you would savor each tiny little bite. Savor your sweet drink that way too. Don't guzzle it down without even tasting it, because then you're consuming an enormous number of calories without extracting full satisfaction from the experience.

Alternatively, you can spruce up your water so you'll enjoy it more. Add a squish of lemon or lime or orange juice to it. Drink carbonated spring water or hot or chilled herbal tea, especially green tea, which is purported to have natural antioxidants and is caffeine-free.

Better yet—drink living water. It's free.

Is It Okay to Eat Sugar?

Over the years, I have heard various lay people argue that sugar is chemically addictive, much in the same way morphine and methamphetamine are addictive. I have also seen lay articles on that subject on the Internet. However, only *one* formal research study is ever cited to support that hypothesis.

It is the rat study I mentioned previously, in which rats were intermittently deprived of food and then refed sugar water.[1] The study showed that food deprivation followed by sugar-water refeeding affected the neurotransmitters in the pleasure center of rats' brains. Since drug addiction is also believed to stimulate the brain's pleasure center, the inference was made that sugar might be chemically addictive, just as those drugs are addictive.

I find that supposition to be interesting but not well supported. The rat study only establishes a correlation or connection between dieting, consuming sugar, and the pleasure center of the brain. It doesn't establish causation. Nor does it *prove* that the altered levels of brain chemicals drive the animal to seek out more and more sugar in a "drug-seeking" type of behavior.

For all we know, the period of fasting the rats were exposed to could be what caused the chemical changes in their brains. But if that were true, it would blow the whole theory that sugar is chemically addictive, and it would support my notion that dieting (periodic fasting) is what is bad for you.

I don't mean to bore you with too much technical information about the rat study, but my point is no research actually proves the theory to be true, especially not in humans. No matter what the lay propaganda on the Internet says, there is no actual scientific research that proves we can become chemically addicted to sugar.

One source of confusion here is that the word *addiction* means different things to different people. If you use the word to describe a habitual, self-destructive behavior, then I would say yes, you're right, consuming sugar can be a highly habit-forming behavior. But notice I didn't say the sugar per se was chemically addictive. I said the behavior of eating the sugar is what you get hooked on.

Why do we become so dependent on the behavior of eating sugar? For one thing, it tastes good. Eating it brings us pleasure. In addition, eating sugar can make us feel better emotionally and physically because it takes away our hunger pangs very quickly. That alone can be a big draw because most of us hate to feel hungry. It makes us feel anxious.

There you go—two valid behavioral reasons why you might want to eat too much sugar: it takes away our hunger pangs almost immediately, and it also tastes good. Do you really need to be chemically addicted to it to explain your behavior? Aren't those two factors enough?

Think about it. When you train a dog to perform a certain behavior by giving it food, you appeal to its pleasure center too. Does that mean the dog is addicted to dog treats? No, it doesn't. It just means that he likes the reward, and therefore he does what he needs to do to get more.

If you go to parties and have too much fun, do you become addicted to having fun? If you get too many presents on your birthday, do you become addicted to getting presents? Where do you draw the line between having an addiction and just being spoiled rotten by having too much pleasure?

What happens is the more pleasure you have, the more you want. It can be true if you're talking about presents, money, sugar, and a lot of other things that press your pleasure button. When it comes to presents, you need bigger and better ones to impress you. When it comes to money, you need more and more to please you. When it comes to éclairs, it takes bigger and sweeter ones to impress you if you eat them every day.

It's not the substance of sugar per se that's good or bad; it's how you consume the substance that determines whether you've used it or abused it. You can abuse any of those things that stimulate your pleasure center, not just sugar. You can even abuse honey, which God gave us for our pleasure in the garden of Eden. Honey is pure sugar, but God gave it to us to enjoy. We are just supposed to think of it as being a precious luxury and consume it properly (in small amounts and when we're hungry).

I suppose that's why God made bees with stingers to guard the honey, so we'd think twice about eating too much of it. It was a built-in reminder to not overdo it.

My point is we must stop blaming the food and start taking responsibility for our pattern of consumption of the food.

To support my stance that being spoiled by sugar is different from being addicted to it, I would like to point out a couple differences between taking addictive drugs and overeating sugar. Remember that I'm subspecialty board-certified in pain management. I regularly prescribe strong narcotics like morphine and methadone to patients, and I regularly screen them for addictive tendencies. I am on familiar ground here.

In order to overcome chemical dependence, you have to completely and entirely stay sober forever. You can't dabble in taking drugs or alcohol. Once you start, you usually can't stop.

Well, at one time, I binged on sugar, and some might therefore have called me chemically addicted to it. But if I were chemically dependent then, I would have to be now as well, and I'm not. Now I can eat only a little sugar and feel satisfied. Explain *that* if sugar is chemically addictive. I shouldn't be able to eat it in moderation.

Additionally, even though you can feel narcotized by a sugar binge, as though you took painkillers, you don't go through withdrawal when you abstain, even if you do get hungry after a while. You may get a slight headache, but in general your body doesn't feel so bad you wish you were dead, like you do when you give up drugs and alcohol.

Rejoice, my friend! That is great news. You don't want to have a chemical chain of bondage that compels you to overeat sweets. You want it to be a learned behavior because then you can unlearn it. That means you can learn to enjoy sweets the way God intended: in small amounts and only when you're hungry, like I advocate on the Eden Diet.

Conclusion

As I explained previously, you no longer need to be afraid of eating delicious, rich food. Not even fried foods or sweets. You just have to discipline yourself when you eat them and eat small amounts infrequently. If you indulge in treats in large amounts or too often, your taste buds may become spoiled, and you are likely to overeat those rich foods and gain weight.

I also explained in this chapter why you are not necessarily better off eating diet food. Manufacturer's claims about diet foods may be false or misleading. The truth is you can lose weight when you eat either fattening or diet food—if you eat them in small amounts and only when your body is physically hungry.

Part Two

The Eden Diet: How to Get Skinny Eating Normal Food

Rediscover
Your Hunger Signals

A good meal ought to begin with hunger.

French proverb

As a physician, I can ask patients about nearly anything. So I ask people about their eating habits—even if they come in with unrelated conditions. I like to find out what the thin people are doing right and what the obese people are doing wrong, mostly so I can copy the behavior of the thin people.

Recently, I surveyed two ladies whom I will call Janine and Tanya. Janine, who was slim, reported eating primarily when she was physically hungry. In contrast, Tanya, who was well over three hundred pounds, reported being more likely to eat in response to nonphysical stimuli, like emotions, automatic habits, and the time on the clock.

In reality Janine and Tanya represent opposite ends of a continuum, with most people falling somewhere in between. However, studying them as extremes can be very helpful. It highlights the differences between the groups and identifies the habits that lead to success.

What habits are worth copying? Just look at what Janine, my slim patient, does. Before she eats, she asks herself, "Am I physically hungry?" When the answer is that she *is* hungry, she follows it up with another question, "How much food do I *need* to eat (not how much do I *want* to eat)?" In other words, if you want to lose weight and keep it off, learn to be more like Janine and wait for hunger, and then eat smaller portions.

You may not realize how those questions can change your life, but I do. They are the same questions that have allowed me to maintain my weight loss for over twenty-five years.

In this chapter, I'll help you get in the habit of asking those critically important questions, and that, in turn, will help you eat less and lose weight.

In the first section of this chapter, I help you to attune to your body's signals so you know when it's appropriate to eat. In the second section, I teach you how to trust your body's ability to help you pick the right foods. In the final section, I help you identify when your body is saying it's had enough — and how to stop eating when it does.

The Internal-External Theory
of Weight Control

I'm not the first medical person to advocate eating according to internal cues (hunger pangs). In 1968, a social psychologist named Dr. Stanley Schacter published a landmark study that clearly showed how obese people eat according to external cues, like the sight or smell of food or the time of day, whereas slim people eat according to their hunger signals.[1]

Dr. Schacter is considered to be a pioneer in the field of obesity research and was one of the rare social scientists ever inducted into the National Academy of Sciences. His work has been cited hundreds if not thousands of times in other research studies. I even remember studying about him twenty years ago when I was at Cornell.

The obvious implication of Dr. Schacter's groundbreaking work is that if you want to be able to lose weight and keep it off, you have to learn to identify and respond properly to your hunger pangs. In other words, if you want to weigh the same as a thin person, you should try to eat for the same reasons she eats.

I'm not sure if Dr. Schacter was a Christian, and I don't know if he'd agree that we should obey our hunger pangs because God gave them to us. However, I'm fairly sure of one thing: if we wanted to lose weight, he'd tell us to stop dieting and simply let our internal signals guide us into thinness.

Personally, I think it's a little embarrassing that we rely on science to tell us to eat according to hunger pangs when God himself made us that way. Do we really need scientists to validate God's original design? Think about it.

Hunger Is Subjective and Infused with Emotion

Hunger, like other types of pain, is a subjective experience. Different people perceive it differently, and different people respond to it differently.

The reason for these differences is biological. To feel pain, you must have functioning nerve endings, neurotransmitters, and a spinal cord and brain. However, there's more to you than your anatomy. You have a mind, emotions, and a spirit too. As such, you experience pain in the context of your thoughts and emotions, not just through your physical nerve endings.

Speaking as a subspecialist in the field of pain management, let me assure you that nonphysical factors (emotions and past experiences) are at least as important as the physical factors in modulating the magnitude—and meaning—of your pain.

People who suffer from insomnia, major life stressors, poor coping skills, or a history of abuse or major trauma seem to tolerate pain poorly compared to people without those conditions. In other words, if you're a stressed-out person who carries a lot of emotional baggage and doesn't sleep well, your hunger pangs may bother you more than they bother the next person.

Likewise, if your brother died from cancer that spread to his back, you might unconsciously fear that your back pain means cancer, and that fear makes your pain seem more intense — even if your pain is due to a muscle spasm rather than a tumor. If you feel that your pain indicates a dangerous condition, it hurts more.

Think about how this relates to hunger. You may have learned from past dieting experiences to doubt your ability to feed yourself properly. "How long will this hunger last?" "What if I overeat and gain all the weight back?" In this scenario, fear robs you of your coping energy, so your hunger seems worse than it actually is.

Of all emotions that modulate the perception of hunger pains, fear appears to be the most prevalent and the most powerful. Isn't fear at the root of stress, anger, and anxiety? I believe it is.

Think about the words some people use to describe their hunger. Their words broadcast fear. Some overweight patients say they're "starving to death," when by just looking at them you can see they're not. *Starving* and *death* are pretty strong, emotion-packed, anxiety- and fear-driven words to describe the feeling you get after not eating for a few hours.

What are they really saying? They're *scared* to death of feeling a tiny bit hungry. They can't tolerate the discomfort, and, on some unconscious level, they fear they might die.

You might argue that it's just a figure of speech, and that I'm reading too much into it. Perhaps. But why not just say, "I'm hungry" when you're hungry? Why say you're "starving to death" if you don't believe it's true on some unconscious level?

If you believe that you're starving to death, hear me now: no matter what the Accuser would like you to believe, you don't need to be afraid of hunger. Hunger pangs are a type of discomfort that is good for you, because hunger reminds you to care for your body by feeding it. Hunger signals were given to you by a loving Creator, who has your best interests in mind. When you feel hunger, it's good news. It means you're going to get to eat something very satisfying very soon!

Attuning to Your Hunger

Despite the individual differences in the perception of hunger, most people describe the sensation as being a pain or as a feeling of hollowness or emptiness. They may feel knotted up or contracted in the upper to middle chest or in the lower throat area, right below the breastbone. They may also describe a churning or rumbling sensation in the stomach that comes in waves.

However, some people experience hunger differently. When they are hungry, they feel jittery, light-headed, irritable, faint, or spacey. They may experience a mild headache or some other vague malaise instead of physical pains over the stomach area.

What about you? What do your hunger pangs feel like? Some people are so out-of-touch with their internal signals that they don't know how to answer this question.

If you're not sure about what hunger feels like, then do a one-time experiment. Eat a light meal—like a small breakfast or lunch—and then wait many, many hours before eating again. Eventually, you should experience uncomfortable sensations that are probably your experience of hunger.

Before I go further, let me clarify. I'm not saying you should wait many, many hours before eating *every time* you eat on this plan. I'm simply saying that if you're out of touch with your internal signals, you need to find them again. And waiting a long time to eat might be what it takes to find your hunger when you first start this program.

It's kind of like starting out in the military with boot camp. Intensive "find your hunger" boot camp. If you don't know what hunger feels like, hold off on eating until you are sure you do know. And then, once you memorize the feeling, carry on with the rest of the plan. That means, subsequently, when you feel true, physical hunger, eat! More precisely, eat with the intense satisfaction and joy that God intended for you.

You must learn to recognize true hunger, so that when you feel it, you'll know how to use it to your advantage. Hunger is like your internal compass. It's a tool. It gives you direction.

You wouldn't go on a hiking trip without first learning how to use your compass or GPS, would you? Of course you wouldn't. You'd get lost without some sort of guidance system. It's the same way with hunger. Learn the nuances of your tool, and you'll be able to use it more effectively.

However, let me be clear. As I mentioned previously, this program is not *about* feeling hungry. It's not about the tool itself. It's about how to use the tool to your advantage. It's about waiting until you're hungry and then feeding yourself properly—with satisfaction and joy and with the right amount and type of food.

Because it's such an important point, I'm going to say it again, and then discuss it even more fully in the next chapter: the Eden Diet is about feeding your hunger to the point of satisfaction, not simply enduring it. As God is my witness, I don't understand how people can hear my instructions and think that I'm trying to promote that people feel hungry all the time, but some still walk away with that perception. I suppose that hunger is such a sensitive subject for them that they don't "hear" anything else I say after the first few words.

Okay, now that I have driven that point home, I'll carry on with what I was saying previously.

If you're trying to memorize what it feels like to be hungry, then when those hunger pangs finally hit you, take a full inventory of how you feel physically. Do you have a headache? Do you feel rumbling in your stomach? Are you dizzy?

Once you grab hold of how you feel, eat a little something and see which of the physical symptoms go away or improve. Whatever physical symptom (or symptoms) improves is your hunger equivalent. For example, if you didn't experience hunger pangs in the stomach area, but felt a slight headache that went away after eating, then a slight headache might be your hunger equivalent. That's how you'll know when you're hungry in the future.

It's also important to notice how you feel emotionally before you eat. Are you anxious or panicked? In other words, do you feel fear, as I alluded to in the prior section? If so, then grab hold of those emotions (which may be lying to you) and remind yourself of the truth. Nothing bad happened just because you experienced mild hunger for a little while! Rather, something very good happened—you learned that you were able to feed that hunger with satisfaction, just like you will do in the future when you feel hungry.

Unless you acknowledge and renounce the lies that accompany your hunger, the lies will continue to govern your eating habits and sabotage your efforts at weight loss.

More will be discussed regarding how emotions tie into eating in chapter 7.

How to Distinguish True Hunger from False Hunger

If you want to lose weight and keep it off permanently, then you have to learn how to distinguish true hunger from false hunger.

As you know, true hunger originates in your body when you actually need to consume food. It's the physiological mechanism that God created in the beginning to ensure survival of the species.

But what is false hunger? Basically, false hunger is a lie that originates in your head. It's when you need or want something intellectually, emotionally, or spiritually, and you're misled into believing food is the thing you're looking for.

False hunger can be generated by unmet emotional needs; boredom; or the sight, smell, taste, or thought of food. It can also be generated in response to advertising and other food-related propaganda such as TV commercials, and in response to sinful desires, such as greed and gluttony.

With true hunger, you're usually not so picky about what you will eat. You'll eat anything to stop the hunger pangs. With false hunger, you may have a strong desire for a specific food. You must have that exact thing, and you can't get it off your mind until you eat it.

The second way to discern true from false hunger is to wait. Notice how your feelings change over time. True hunger comes and goes in waves, with each successive wave increasing slightly in intensity. Waves start out widely spaced but become closer together and more intense if they are not fed. In a way, they're like watered-down labor pains, increasing in strength each time a wave of contraction hits.

On the other hand, false hunger doesn't cycle up and down the way real stomach contractions do. False hunger hits you abruptly and then levels off. When it's not fed, it generally decreases in intensity over time, unlike true hunger pangs, which increase.

The third test is to notice the pattern of the onset of your feelings. True hunger usually starts very subtly with mild sensations in the stomach. It typically starts about three to five hours after your last meal (depending on what and how much of it you ate) and slowly builds up over a period of hours.

False hunger, as previously mentioned, starts very abruptly and is associated with a strong urge or impulse to eat. It often escalates quickly in the first few minutes of your noticing the desire. False hunger also tends to strike when you feel emotional (depressed, bored, lonely, angry, and so forth) or because of habit or at the sight, smell, or thought of food.

A fourth way to discern true from false hunger is to notice what you were doing when the thought first hit you. If you're busy and interested in something, true hunger pangs may annoy you because you don't want to stop what you're doing. For example, you may be having so much fun painting a picture you don't want to stop to eat.

On the other hand, false hunger may strike because you don't want to continue what you're doing. For example, you may feel frustrated that you can't balance your checkbook, so you get up to make a sandwich.

Numerous other reasons may cause you to experience false hunger. For example, you may simply have a need to chew. Chewing when you're nervous is no different from repetitively clicking a pen or tapping your feet when you're nervous. Back when I was in college, my obesity research mentor Dr. Levitsky called those behaviors "stereo-tic." Even rats did them when they were stressed. If you like to engage in motor activity when you're nervous, consider squeezing a stress ball with your hand or doing some other form of repetitive activity that doesn't require you to swallow unnecessary food.

False hunger might also originate from a desire to have a flavor in your mouth. You might call this feeling "mouth-hunger." In that case, you might try chewing gum or eating sugar-free mints. You get flavor for fewer calories that way. Or, better yet, stop putting substances in your mouth when you're not actually hungry. Find a diversion like cleaning out your car, and forget about your mouth.

It's also possible that you may have incorrectly interpreted your other bodily signals as being hunger signals. Perhaps you were thirsty and confused that sensation with hunger. Maybe you heard or felt gas rumbling around in your intestines and thought it was hunger pangs. Maybe you felt tired and reflexively reached for food to "refuel." Or perhaps your appetite was stimulated by certain medications.

Finally, you might have false hunger from an unmet emotional need. You'll hear more about that in chapter 7. In those cases you might think you're hungry, but you might decide that no food sounds appetizing. That should be the first clue that what you need isn't in the kitchen. When you're really, really hungry, you don't care what you eat.

How to Become Distracted So You Eat Less

If you feel the very beginnings of hunger, don't panic. You don't have to make a beeline to the fridge to prevent the next tiny little hunger pang. Nothing bad will happen if you sit with the feeling for a while and let it grow. If it's real hunger, the pangs will go away in a short while and then come back a little later and a little stronger.

During that waiting time, look for a healthy activity to distract you. Read and memorize Scripture. Pray for somebody who needs help. Pray for your family and your friends. Even pray for your enemies.

Write down the revelations God gives you as you read this book. Write about your successes and what you learn from your failures.

Alternatively, do something mundane but important. Clean out your purse. Vacuum your car. Wash your windows. Do laundry. Rearrange your sock drawer. Or vacuum your socks. It almost doesn't matter what you do. Just get your mind on something outside of yourself.

(The only exception is ironing. If you are faced with a situation where you have to pick between ironing and eating, definitely eat. In that situation, it doesn't even matter if you're hungry. Ironing is a vile activity and should be avoided at all costs.)

Seriously, to ensure that you engage in more meaningful activities than sock vacuuming and ironing-aversive eating, you may decide to compile a daily to-do list. Include not only your necessary chores on that list but also things you can do to pamper yourself. Don't forget to put exercise and socializing on your list. Too much work and not enough play make Jane a dull girl.

Understand When It Is Time to Eat
(the Apple Test and Other Ways to Rate Your Hunger)

The Apple Test is a very simple technique that can help you decide when it's time to eat.

The premise of the test is that when you're physically hungry, you'll eat anything—even an apple.

To take the Apple Test, do the following. If you crave a particular food, like cheesecake, imagine it sitting on a plate next to a beautiful, shiny, perfect, bright red apple. Ask yourself, "Am I hungry enough to eat the apple?" If the answer is no, you don't get to eat the cheesecake. You may want the cheesecake, but you're not actually physically hungry for it.

Let me be clear. I'm not saying that you "should" eat the apple if you "would" eat the apple, or that apples are right to eat and cheesecake is wrong to eat. I'm simply saying that if you wouldn't eat the apple at that point, you're not physically hungry.

Proverbs 27:7 says it this way, "One who is full loathes honey from the comb, but to the hungry even what is bitter tastes sweet." Voila! The Bible actually tells you how to discern true, physical hunger from other hungers. You know you're hungry when you'd eat something nasty to stop the hunger pangs.

Hey, maybe I'm not as mean as you thought. At least I told you to eat a boring food rather than a nasty food. I could have made you take the Bitter Lemon Test instead of the Apple Test.

As I said, if you wouldn't eat the apple, you get no food, period. No cheesecake, no apples, no honey from the comb, no bitter lemons, nothing. However, that doesn't mean that you *never* get cheesecake. If you're in the mood for cheesecake, just wait a little while longer and take the Apple Test again, after your hunger has had a chance to grow. Eventually, you'll be hungry enough to eat the apple, and that's when you get cheesecake! (However, don't be surprised if your thoughts move on to some other food by then.)

The Apple Test doesn't work for everybody. Some people love apples so much that they crave them and even binge on them. Those people must substitute a food that they perceive as neutral or boring, like celery or crackers. Those people could modify the test so that it becomes the Celery Test.

Still other people hate apples. For them, it becomes the Banana Test (if they're neutral to bananas and find them boring). You get the idea. Pick a food that bores you, not one that you hate. If you're hungry enough to eat a boring food, you're hungry enough to eat the food you truly desire.

If the Apple Test doesn't work for you, there's a second option for rating your hunger. You can rate it as mild, moderate, or severe, depending on how easy or hard it is to distract yourself from the sensation.

If you are only mildly hungry, then it should be relatively easy to become distracted from your hunger by engaging in other activities. Turn on some music or call a friend, and see if your hunger pangs go away. If you are only marginally hungry, then your hunger will probably go away and come back a little stronger a little later on.

In contrast, if you are moderately hungry, then it should be harder to become distracted and stay that way, because your hunger pangs keep penetrating your thoughts.

When you are mildly or moderately hungry—in other words, if you would eat the apple—or if you find it harder to become distracted because your hunger keeps interrupting you, go ahead and eat. Eat whatever you like—just enough food so you just barely begin to feel the food in your stomach—just enough food to quiet the hunger pangs for a few hours until your next meal.

Try not to wait until you are extremely hungry, though, or your anxiety may lead you to overeat. I mentioned it previously, but it's important and is worth repeating. Don't go hungry for too long. Eat when you're mildly to moderately hungry. If you'd eat the apple, you're ready to eat the food you desire. If you wait too long, you may become extremely hungry, and you may end up overeating from sheer panic.

If the rating scale based on distracting yourself doesn't work, and if you're unable to use either the Apple Test or the notion of mild or moderate hunger to guide your eating, then I have a third option for you. It's also based on Proverbs 27:7, and is called the "Unsweetened Chocolate Test." Unsweetened chocolate is nasty. If you'd eat that, you're definitely hungry. Hey, don't blame me—you brought it on yourself by being difficult.

Why Does Hunger Build Up over Time?

My friend Tiffany has a theory about why hunger comes and goes and eventually builds up over time. She thinks that the slow buildup allows us time to collect food and prepare for the meal.

Previously, we didn't have freezers and microwave ovens. It took hours to collect and prepare our food. Once upon a time, a tiny, beginning hunger pang served as an excellent reminder to start the lengthy and inconvenient meal-preparation process.

Perhaps that's indirect evidence that we shouldn't eat at the very beginning of our hunger. We should wait awhile and let our hunger grow, just as God had us do when we had to work harder to prepare our meals.

Let Waiting Be Your Offering

In 1 Corinthians 10:31, Paul said that we should do everything (including eating and drinking) to the glory of God. Since we are told to do *everything* to the glory of God, that means we should wait to eat for his glory, as well. Waiting shows how much we trust the internal signals he gave us, how we love and respect the bodies he gave us, and how we are willing to discipline ourselves for his glory.

Instead of withholding food for long periods of time as you might on a regular fast, however, I'm asking you only to withhold it for a shorter time, just until you reach the point of mild to moderate hunger. That may mean you have to wait for another twenty minutes before you would eat the apple, or it might mean you have to wait for two or three hours. Either way, the act of waiting takes self-discipline, and it's a beautiful offering to God.

God expects you to give to him according to your ability. Do you remember the widow who gave her last copper coins to the synagogue? Even though her offering was worth only a fraction of a penny, it represented a greater sacrifice, relatively speaking, than those of the rich Pharisees who gave 10 percent of their extra fat (Mark 12:41–44).

Give to God that which you are able to give, and he will receive it with great joy. If you're just beginning to break out of bondage to food, then waiting an extra twenty minutes to let your hunger grow to a mild to moderate level may be a real sacrifice for you. If so, then it will be extra special to God.

Fight Fire with Fire

During the time you wait for your hunger to build, you might be unsure of yourself. You might ask, "How about now? Is now the right time for me to eat?"

If you're not very physically hungry but feel the urge to eat for emotional or other reasons, handle the temptation as Jesus did. When Satan told Jesus to change the stones to loaves of bread, Jesus responded with Scripture, not willpower, saying, "It is written: 'Man does not live on bread alone, but on every word that comes from the mouth of God'" (Matthew 4:4 NIV).

The Bible says, "Submit yourselves, then, to God. Resist the devil, and he will flee from you" (James 4:7). The Bible doesn't tell you to resist the Devil on your own; it says to submit to God to be able to resist him. Jesus, in his time of greatest temptation, called on God and on Scripture for backup. You should rely on him too. Quote Scripture, pray, and meditate, and you will be able to resist the temptation to eat prematurely.

Thank God for Hunger

Whether or not you feel like doing it, thank God for giving you hunger pangs. Realize that they are useful sensations given to you by a loving Creator who has your best interests in mind. Thank him for letting you identify them. Pray that he'll help change your attitude about them so you appreciate them.

If you've stretched out your stomach from years of overeating, you especially need to embrace your hunger as a good thing. Understand those pains for what they are: the sign that your stomach is shrinking back to the size it should be. So tolerate the hunger pangs for a little while before you eat—wait until the apple sounds good to you, and then eat. As I said, consider it an act of worship to wait, and thank God for the discipline that lets you do it.

Your Body Will Tell You What It Needs

In the beginning, Adam's body was made in the image of God (Genesis 1:26), which means he must have been physically perfect. I suppose intrinsic perfection is why he had the opportunity to live forever if he had only eaten from the right trees (Genesis 3:22).

If Adam was designed for eternal life, then he needed the ability to self-heal in case he was injured. Surely he would have scraped himself against a jagged rock in the garden or maybe fallen out of a tree and broken a bone. Eternity is a long time to not get hurt.

Even before Adam acquired self-consciousness at the Fall, his body would have been fully capable of taking care of itself. In fact, I'll take it one step further and say that his body might even have been better able to take care of itself without self-consciousness to override its internal programming and get it into trouble.

Even today we see the remnants of the body's original intelligent programming. If we have a cut, we clot. If a cell dies in our body, our white blood cells "eat" them to clear the debris. If we break a bone, we grow it back together. And we do it without thinking. If we had to think about it, we'd probably mess it up.

By intelligent design, your blueprints for healing and your blueprints for weight loss were hardwired into you in the beginning, and they are still accessible to you. In the case of healing from your obesity, you just have to learn how to relax your intellectual desire to control, submit your hunger pangs to God, and let the healing begin.

The Body's Self-Healing Power as Manifested in My Pain Management Practice

If you could see what I see as a doctor, you would believe the body has built-in intelligence to heal itself, and you would trust your internal signals. This includes your hunger pangs.

The body's self-healing capacity flows out of us most unmistakably when I perform a certain type of osteopathic manipulation similar to chiropractic, but without the cracking. It's called a functional indirect technique, and it was taught to me by my teachers and dear friends Micha Sale, PT, and Ed Stiles, DO. Both are pioneers in this type of manipulation and are widely respected by anyone "in the know" in their field.

To utilize Dr. Stiles's manipulation maneuver, you first have to identify the joints and soft tissues that are restricted from moving normally. Then you have to position the body part in a very specific way and have the patient completely relax as you support his or her weight. Next, you apply a very gentle compressive or distractive force through the abnormal area, in accordance with what the tissue tension "tells you" as you monitor it with your hand.

What happens next is absolutely amazing. As long as the patient is fully relaxed, the affected body part visibly and sometimes dramatically twists and turns itself as the tissue tension unwinds. Patients think I am moving them, but their own body causes the movement.

The movement is thought by the experts to be due to the tissue memory stored in the part of the brain known as the limbic system. All I know is that it reminds me of the way the tension in an old-fashioned coiled telephone cord unwinds when you suspend the receiver in midair.

The body is brilliant and knows exactly how to unwind its tissue tension using its preprogrammed healing software; however, it can't start unwinding its way back to normal unless it is positioned in a state of complete relaxation in the arms of the doctor or therapist.

In the case of weight loss, you tap into healing the same way. You have to relinquish control and fully relax in the arms of the One who is trying to help you. If you continue to micromanage your eating based on your worldly knowledge rather than submit to your God-given hunger pangs, you won't be able to relax and unwind toward your cure.

The Home Alone Phenomenon

If you saw the movie *Home Alone*, you have already seen an example of how the body can right itself concerning food. The main character, a young boy, was inadvertently left behind when his family went on vacation. When he realized he was home alone, he panicked. However, he soon realized that, with his parents gone, he had a chance to be naughty. He pigged out on junk food, watched questionable television, and stayed up too late at night.

Not long into the party, however, he became physically ill because of what he'd eaten. After eating all that junk food, his body screamed for nutritious food. Consequently, the boy straightened up, shopped for groceries, and prepared a well-balanced, nutritious meal with vegetables and meat.

You see, the little boy only binged on junk food because he knew he would never have gotten to do it if his parents had been home. He wanted what was forbidden. However, when he discovered how it made him feel, the novelty wore off. He literally *came to his senses* and started listening to his body again.

The story reminds me of the parable of the prodigal son. He indulged himself in worldly ways but eventually listened to his inner voice. "When he came to his senses, he said, 'How many of my father's hired men have food to spare, and here I am starving to death!'" (Luke 15:17 NIV).

When the Prodigal Son came to his senses, he returned home to his father. This is what your body will do. After you've had your fill of junk food, your body will come to its senses too and will crave healthy food.

I can relate to how the main character in *Home Alone* felt after his junk-food splurge. Sometimes I really just want to devour a chocolate bar or ice cream sundae or some chips and queso instead of having a real meal. However, at the next meal, my body usually comes to its senses and craves something nutritious, like a turkey sandwich or a grilled chicken salad.

Think Less and Feel More

I like to think of myself as a fairly intelligent person. That's why it was hard for me to accept that my body could be smarter than my brain when it comes to knowing how I am supposed to eat. You could say it hurt my pride. But eventually, I became convinced by the compulsive eating books that I had no choice. So I relaxed my conscious control over what I ate, and I began to listen to my body's internal signals. It worked great. I lost weight right away and felt better emotionally, too.

This is how I did it: I started by making the decision to pay attention to my bodily signals. Then I noticed that when I ate a particularly sugary meal, at the next meal I craved protein. One day I wanted vegetables more than anything, but another day I craved high-fat foods. If I craved cookies, then several hours later, when I was hungry again, I asked myself which sounded better: more cookies or a piece of meat and some vegetables. When I did this, I actually found that the prospect of eating meat and vegetables sounded better than the prospect of eating more cookies. It was shocking, but true.

In the same way, if I ate half a veggie sandwich with cheese and corn chips one day for lunch but skipped the meat and fruit, then soon enough I'd crave meat and fruit. Sometimes it took days for my cravings to register, but then all I'd want was meat and fruit for a couple days in a row.

I also found that some days I wanted what my thin friend Tammy calls "backward dinner," where you eat dessert first, or you eat only dessert and skip the entrée altogether. However, after that kind of meal, which has no nutritional value, I would always want something really healthy for my next meal, like a grilled chicken salad and fruit. It was God's perfect plan to ensure my health.

Yes, I'm saying that I learned how to trust my bodily sensations through trial and error and by paying attention to how I felt physically. But also it was like my faith in God. It was something I just couldn't explain and still can't. Sometimes I would just know things, like that I needed protein. And I assume God is the one who put that information into my head because I don't know how else it got there.

I'm basically saying that you're going to have to tune out the worldly dieting dogma that clutters your brain. Instead, you need to tune in to your bodily sensations. I'm saying you have to stop thinking so much. Instead, allow yourself to feel more of your physical sensations. And have faith that God will put the message in your head when you need to eat healthy food.

Believe It or Not, You'll Crave Healthy Food

One day I was trying to figure out what I wanted for breakfast. I was alone, since my husband had taken the kids fishing. I had a rare opportunity to do what I wanted, including maybe even get a special treat for breakfast instead of my usual fare.

I ran through the list of my favorite breakfast foods. I thought about my favorite blueberry doughnut from my favorite doughnut shop. No, that wasn't what I wanted. Then I thought of my favorite cinnamon-chip scone from my favorite coffee shop. No, that wasn't it either. I finally realized that what I wanted was just the cut-up cantaloupe that I had in the fridge, with a cup of coffee with creamer, sugar, and hazelnut flavoring.

I actually preferred cantaloupe over pastries. But the pastries were okay for me too. You see, I know I can have a doughnut or scone anytime I am hungry. I just didn't want it at that moment.

Don't feel that you have to get the doughnut in life just because you know you can. Sometimes your body actually wants the cantaloupe! In other words, accept the attitude transformation when God gives it to you, and trust your body when it tells you to eat healthy food.

How to Know When to Stop Eating

What does fullness feel like? Usually, fullness is felt as a vague but not uncomfortable physical presence in the middle of one's lower chest or upper stomach, in the same place where hunger pangs are felt.

However, unlike hunger pangs, fullness signals are harder to identify. Unless you overly stuff yourself, they don't hurt, they don't make you feel anxious the way hunger pangs do, and they don't make noise. Therefore, it's harder to notice them if they're only mild in intensity.

Fullness clearly means different things to different people. To some people, fullness is when they barely perceive a mild stretch in the stomach, and to others it's when they feel bloated and sick and can't eat another bite. Where do you fall on that spectrum?

Now consider the relationship between fullness and satisfaction.

If you fill up on large quantities of bland diet food so you can escape your hunger pangs, you may still feel dissatisfied and empty. You might even binge on other food later on to appease your dissatisfaction. Think about it. Wouldn't you feel more satisfied by a small steak and a small serving of vegetables with real butter than by an enormous salad that tasted like Styrofoam? Fullness and sensory satisfaction go hand in hand.

In other words, if you eat delicious, pretty food that smells good, you will feel more satisfied and full. That's why chefs say you first eat with your eyes and then with your mouth and stomach.

Finally, consider other factors that contribute to fullness. If you eat because you perceive a void in your life, not realizing it's a spiritual or emotional void, you might never feel full. You might be a bottomless pit. No matter how much delicious food you eat, you still feel empty because you haven't addressed the real empty space that drives you to eat.

As you have seen, many factors confound the interpretation of fullness. However, let's not throw out the baby with the bathwater just yet. In the next section, I show you how you can use your fullness signals in spite of their drawbacks.

How to Use Your Fullness Signals

If you understand their limitations, you can learn to use fullness signals to help you control your weight. First, you must eat slowly if you're listening for them. It takes at least twenty minutes for fullness signals to register in your brain. If you eat too quickly, you will stuff more food into your stomach than your body actually needs. You must eat slowly so you can give your fullness signals a chance to catch up.

Second, you must pay close attention to how your body feels as you eat. This means you can't be too engrossed in conversation or distracted by other environmental stimuli during your meal, or you will miss the sensation of fullness when it begins.

Once you barely begin to feel fullness signals, stop eating. It doesn't matter if you have eaten less than you think you should eat. Stop eating anyway. Probably, over the next few minutes, you will begin to feel even more food in your stomach as your body catches up and realizes the volume you ate.

You must adopt a new definition for fullness. Previously, you may have eaten until you couldn't eat another bite. You may have called that bloated, uncomfortable feeling "fullness." But now you stop eating as soon as you first become aware of the sensation of food in your stomach.

You want to lose weight, right? Then you have to eat much less food than you had been accustomed to in the past.

You Have to Shrink Your Stomach

Will the right portion size lead you to feel comfortably "full"? Surprisingly, the answer is, "Not at first."

If you habitually overate in the past, then your stomach is likely to be stretched out and numb. Therefore, it is important for you to eat small portions of food so it can shrink down to a more normal size. Soon your stomach will be better able to sense the small portions of food you put in it, and it will be more likely to tell you it's full.

Why is it important to let your stomach shrink to a normal size? It takes more food to fill up a stretched-out stomach than it takes to fill a normal-size stomach. If you eat until you're full with a stretched-out stomach, you'll simply be taking in too many calories to lose weight, especially if you eat medium- or high-calorie food, like cheesecake.

That's why it's important to allow yourself to feel hungry several times a day. When you are hungry, a wonderful thing is happening. Your stomach is shrinking back down to the size God intended for it to be in the beginning.

How Much Food Is Enough?

I would like to offer two approaches to estimate the amount you should eat. The first method is the better one to use when you are first starting out on this program. It consists of waiting until you feel hungry and then eating portions about half the amount of food you ate previously, regardless of the type of food you are eating.

Easy, right? If you normally eat a double meat and cheese extra value combo meal, go ahead and order that again, but eat only half of it. You can save the rest for your next meal. Or you could just order less food. If you normally order the large combo meal, order a kid's meal instead. Or just get a regular burger and water. Or just fries and water. Try ordering only *one* individual food item instead of the entire combo meal, or order one or two small items off of the dollar menu, depending on how hungry you are.

The second approach is a little more stringent and might be easier for you to adopt later on in the Eden Diet. Here it is: eat a meal that, if you were to lump it all together, would be about the size of your closed fist. I said *your* fist, not Goliath's. Or maybe two fists.

The second approach takes a little more discipline to follow, and I think you know why. A fist-size quantity is a small amount of food. However, on the upside, you get to eat frequently, and you get to eat whatever you want. If you get hungry every three hours, then eat every three hours. If you eat two fists full and don't get hungry for five or six hours, that's fine too. Just make sure you're hungry before you eat again.

Understand that the fist rule is just a starting point. I am not able to give you exact guidelines about how much you should eat because I have no idea how much food your body needs. Only your body can know something like that. It would be presumptuous and arrogant for me to think otherwise. Do I know more than God working in you through your hunger pangs? I don't think so.

Finally, remember to trust whichever signal comes first, whether it is the beginning sensation of food in your stomach or the visual cue that you've eaten one or two fists full of food.

Other Factors That Affect How Much You Should Eat

The amount you should eat varies depending on the type of food you choose to eat. If you eat cheesecake, which is very, very calorie dense, then you'll need to eat a smaller volume of it than if you were eating melon. I'm not saying you should count your calories—just be aware that certain foods are more calorie dense than others, and they should be eaten in smaller quantities.

In other situations you can actually eat more than this and not gain weight. If you are very muscular, for instance, you can probably eat more than a fist-size quantity and still lose weight. The reason is that muscles burn more calories than fat. The more lean body mass (muscles) you have, the higher your basal metabolic rate and the more calories you can consume without gaining weight.

In addition, if you exercise regularly, you can also eat more without gaining weight because you're burning off the excess during and even after exercise.

And if you're very hungry, you should probably eat more than if you are slightly hungry, because your body is asking you for more food. Maybe you need *two* fist-size portions of food, and that's okay too.

Even two fist-size portions of food is a reasonably small amount—so long as you wait until you are truly hungry before you eat. It might take you longer to lose weight that way, but who cares? Sometimes slow and steady wins the race.

As you might expect, it takes practice to estimate your portion size properly. If you guess wrong and eat too little, the worst thing that will happen is your body will figure it out and tell you to eat again sooner rather than later. If you guess wrong and eat too much, you will probably stay full longer. It's no big deal either way, so long as you rely on your hunger pangs to initiate eating at your subsequent meal.

Why eat such small portions? Maybe you're thinking, "Half orders? Child's meals? Fist-size portions? What does this woman expect of me?" Well, I hear you. But here's the deal: this is a *weight reduction* plan. If you want to lose weight, you simply have to eat smaller portions of food. That's just the way it is, my friend.

Over time, as you eat smaller meals, you will probably find that your attitudes about portion sizes change as well. You'll adopt healthier attitudes about how much you should eat. Your expectations will reset at a new, normal level. You'll undergo a renewing of the mind regarding how much food you need to eat.

It's hard to think about eating smaller portion sizes. But you have a decision to make. Either you need to learn to feel okay about eating less, or you need to learn to feel okay about being overweight. Which will *you* choose?

Research on Fullness Signals

Physiologically, your fullness signals are imprecise. They only give you a ballpark idea of when to stop eating. I know that firsthand because of a research project I was involved in twenty-some years ago at Cornell. I was fortunate to work with Dr. David Levitsky and his doctoral student Lauren Lissner on the connection between dietary fat and caloric intake.[2] I was Lauren's undergraduate lab helper. I did the chemical testing to determine how many calories were in each of the foods used in the study.

In that study, the subjects were divided into three groups, but they all ate their meals together in the dining room of the research building. If the meal was pasta, the first group got the low-fat version, the second got the medium-fat version, and the third got the high-fat version.

Subjects in all groups were allowed to eat ad libitum in every phase of the experiment, which means that they were allowed to eat as much or as little as they pleased. They could either leave food on their plate or ask for seconds. However, the quantities of food that they consumed were carefully weighed, so as to calculate their exact calorie and fat intake in all phases of the study. This flexible design allowed the subjects to consume more food if they felt hungrier or consume less food if they felt less hungry at different times during the experiment.

Each phase of the study lasted two weeks. If the subject was on the low-fat leg of the study, they ate the low-fat diet for two weeks straight. If they were on the medium-fat leg, they ate that diet for two weeks straight, and so forth. None of the subjects knew what the study was about or that their foods had different fat and calorie contents.

The study showed that when the subjects ate lower-calorie, lower-fat food, they unknowingly made adjustments and ate larger volumes of food at their subsequent meals, presumably because they felt hungrier. Conversely, if they ate higher-calorie food, they made adjustments at subsequent meals and unknowingly ate smaller volumes of food because they were less hungry. However, they didn't adjust perfectly. They lost weight during their two weeks on the low-fat diet and gained weight when they were on the high-fat diet.

In other words, the study showed that their bodies were imprecise when it came to regulating the amount of food they needed according to the volume of food they ate. Their bodies adjusted a little bit to the calorie content of their meals, but not all the way.

This study shows that you shouldn't rely too heavily on your stomach to tell you when to stop eating. If you feel fullness signals, stop eating, but if you don't feel them and you've already eaten one or two fist-size quantities of food, stop eating anyway! If you undershoot how much you should eat, you'll get hungry again sooner rather than later. Then you can eat more. It's simple.

More recently, Dr. Wansink wrote a book that collated his research on how environmental factors affect the way we eat. It's called *Mindless Eating: Why We Eat More Than We Think*.[3] In his book Dr. Wansink showed that his subjects were very susceptible to environmental stimuli that confounded their ability to stop eating at the right time. In other words, he proved that they ate more when they were distracted.

For example, his subjects ate more "all you can eat" chicken wings in a restaurant when the waiter cleared their empty plates from the table. And other subjects ate larger quantities of soup when they unknowingly ate from a "magic" bowl that was rigged to refill itself via hidden tubing.

His subjects also misjudged portion sizes. They ate more food when they ate it straight out of the box compared to when they ate portions out of serving bowls. They ate 14 percent less food when they put their whole serving on one plate compared to when they could go back for seconds and thirds. And they ate less food when they used smaller plates and utensils or when they were alone.

Pooling all of the above research, Dr. Wansink recommended the following in his book: eat food directly off of your plate rather than out of the container, eat off of smaller plates, and pay attention while you eat, especially if you're eating with other people or in an environment with other distractions. He also recommended filling half of your plate with vegetables and then filling the rest of the plate with other things you enjoy. Try it if you want to. It's slightly different than what I recommend, but it still seems reasonable.

The Food Composition Matters

As mentioned previously, it takes at least twenty minutes for the food you eat to even begin to cause satiety. If you scarf down food too quickly, then by the time you feel full you probably will have eaten too much.

In general, sugar from the food you eat enters your bloodstream and causes satiety first, followed by protein and finally fats. The latter two cause the release of a chemical known as cholecystokinin, which acts on the brain to cause satiety.

If you eat a high-fat food, you won't feel full until a long time after you eat it, but you will stay full longer. Conversely, if you eat a high-carbohydrate food, it will curb your hunger more quickly, but the effect will not last as long. That's especially true if the carbohydrate you're eating is table sugar. Table sugar (sucrose) causes a faster, higher blood-sugar spike than the natural sugar you find in fruit (fructose).

I've been asked if eating rice, which is a complex carbohydrate, is what causes you to feel hungry again quickly after eating Chinese food. However, I don't think the high carbohydrate nature of the meal is the entire reason for the rapid return in hunger, unless of course you ate only a small number of calories of the food. I've felt hungry soon after *overeating* Chinese food too. The reason may be the MSG (monosodium glutamate). It's added to food as a flavor enhancer, but, according to a study by Rogers, Blundell, and others, MSG acts on the satiety center of the brain to stimulate your appetite.[4] Gasp!

That means that you should be careful when you use seasoned salt or any product that claims to be a flavor enhancer. It usually contains MSG and could stimulate your appetite and make you fat.

I think it serves us right. Don't you see how spoiled we've become? What's wrong with the food in its natural state, without flavor enhancers? Nowadays everything needs to be bigger and better and more delicious for us to feel satisfied.

But I digress. My main point is that if you eat a high-fat food, you just have to make extra sure you savor it fully and eat small quantities, because it will take the longest to register in your bloodstream. If you eat a high-sugar food, you should realize it will quickly curb your appetite, but your satisfaction may be short lived. And if you eat a high-fiber food, you shouldn't eat excessive quantities just because it is low in calories, or it will expand and stretch your stomach.

Conclusion

One of your first challenges on the Eden Diet is to attune to your bodily sensations of hunger and fullness. You need to realize hunger is not a bad thing and learn to trust it as a natural instinct given by God. Embrace your hunger and learn to wait for it, trust it, and feed it in small portions to the glory of God.

When it comes to fullness signals, know that you might not be able to use them until your stomach shrinks down to a more normal size. Even when your stomach does shrink, your fullness signals may not be fully reliable. You might have to continue using your eyeballs to define a reasonable amount to eat.

In the meantime, continue to use the "fist-size" and "eat half" guidelines. Eating small portions will allow you to become hungry more frequently. This will not only give your stomach lots of opportunities to shrink, but it will also show you that you are capable of feeling satisfied each and every time you eat.

5

Less Food, More Joy

Never eat more than you can lift.

Miss Piggy

Like most women, I like gifts that come in small packages. I especially like dangly, interesting-looking earrings with purple or blue gemstones set in silver. My birthday is in May. Hint. Hint.

But, alas, there is also a downside to getting jewelry. Since it's expensive, when I get it, it's usually my only present, and it leaves the spoiled little child in me wanting more. It stirs up my desire for even bigger presents—ones in big boxes with pretty bows on top. It doesn't even matter much what's inside the big boxes. My inner child craves quantity, not quality.

But then the adult part of my conscience speaks up. It says, "Now, Rita, you know that the best gifts come in small packages. Cherish that gift because it's very special. Quality is more important than quantity." My inner child hates that adult voice.

There you go. I'm admitting that I'm schizophrenic. I'm two conflicted people living in one head, and I hear voices.

What I'm really saying is: there's a never-ending battle in my mind between what I want and what I need. And it's the same story when it comes to food and eating. There's a childlike voice in my mind, and it tells me to do things like eat a hot-fudge sundae for taste, even when I'm not hungry. Meanwhile, the adult voice beats down that child and says I should wait a couple hours until my body needs food.

Yes, I'm also saying there's child abuse going on in my head. My adult voice beats down the voice of the spoiled-rotten little crying child. Maybe I should press charges.

One Sunday my pastor told a great story about this inner conflict. He talked about a Native American man who was torn inside, as I am at times. The man described the battle in his head as being like a fight between two dogs. When he was asked which dog won, the good dog or the bad dog, the man said it was the one he fed.

In my case, this means the more I indulge my inner child (by feeding it sugar, for example), the more it rants and raves to be indulged further and in bigger ways. The more my child gets, the more it wants. I could become a bottomless sugar-and-gift pit if I'm not careful.

Therefore, I have to exercise self-discipline. When I indulge and eat a sweet or greasy, rich, delicious food, like an éclair, I try to remember the difference between the amount of food I want and the amount of food my body actually needs.

And then I have to not eat an éclair again for a while. I go through éclair withdrawal, so that my taste buds settle back down to normal—whatever that is. Otherwise it would take bigger, more delicious, and sweeter éclairs to excite me the next time.

On the Eden Diet, I want to show you how to have the same attitude about éclairs and other rich, delicious food you have when you get an expensive piece of jewelry. I want you to learn to feel more satisfied eating less food in the right way. You'll see that it feels better to eat small quantities of food with satisfaction and entitlement than it does to eat larger quantities of food and be left with a sense of emptiness or guilt.

Get in the Right Frame of Mind:
Eat the Éclair to the Glory of God

Paul suggests in 1 Corinthians 10:31 that we should eat "for the glory of God," but what does that mean in practical terms? It means we should follow the four rules God gave us in the Bible about how to eat. We should eat properly as an act of worship and reverence, just as Jesus did, with thankfulness in mind, peace and joy in our heart, and hunger in our stomach.

Regarding which foods are fit to be eaten, all food is allowable. Even though the Old Testament outlined all kinds of rules about what we could or could not eat, Jesus came along later and released us from the Law. He declared all food fit to be eaten in Mark 7:14–19.

The apostle Paul also wrote about this subject in 1 Corinthians 8. He said, referring to meat offered to idols, that our attitude about food determined if we were sinning when we ate it. If we ate the meat knowing with complete certainty that the Baal statue was just a little action figure, then we would not be sinning when we ate the meat offered to it.

Hear me now: when Jesus and Paul told us that all food was fit to be eaten, they didn't put a clause in the Scripture that gave fat people a separate menu to follow. They never once said that if a person is overweight, he or she must constantly eat diet food or be on a diet.

In other words, the idea that heavy people are morally obligated to lose weight or eliminate certain foods from their diet was not written in the Bible; it was written in the world. And you know what that means. It means Satan probably had something to do with it.

We should embrace our God-given right to eat reasonable portions of any kind of food when we're hungry, even if we are overweight. We are God's beloved children, after all, no matter how big or how small we are.

Our Father in heaven wouldn't restrict any of us from eating when we're hungry any more than we would give our own children a stone when they ask for bread. He just doesn't want us to be gluttonous and eat large quantities of food we don't need, because it's bad for us to do that.

All food is on the "allowed" list for us, and we should not feel guilty when we eat delicious food in small portions when we're hungry. God allows us sensual pleasure in other ways without guilt, so why should we feel guilty when we eat in the way he intended?

Should we feel guilty when we look at a beautiful sunset? Should we feel guilty when we smell the beautiful fragrance of a flower? Should we feel guilty when we hear a beautiful symphony? Should we feel guilty when we enjoy sex with our spouse? Of course we shouldn't. Then why do we feel guilty when we taste sensual pleasure?

I hope that gives you the right perspective.

Eating "with" vs. "for" Satisfaction

I believe there is a difference between eating "with" satisfaction and eating "for" satisfaction." To eat "with" satisfaction denotes a *mind-set*, whereas to eat "for" satisfaction denotes a *pursuit*.

People who know how to eat "with" satisfaction generally don't feel guilt or shame if they eat fattening food. They eat with a mind-set of joy and thankfulness, thinking of the food as a lavish gift from God, and that mindset leads to greater psychological and emotional satisfaction from the eating experience.

On the other hand, some people who eat "for" satisfaction can be bottomless pits for food. That's especially true for emotional eaters. They feel bad deep-down, so they eat large portions of food for pleasure and for a momentary distraction from their ill feelings.

Satisfaction is a relative thing—a subjective perception. That's why it's potentially dangerous to tell emotional eaters to "Eat as much as you want, until you're satisfied." What if their idea of satisfaction is no longer feeling angry or depressed? How much food will they require to feel satisfied in that case? A whole box of chocolate? What kind of reducing diet is that?

Clearly, people who have trouble separating emotional from physical hunger can have a hard time with this concept of "eating for satis-faction." That's why I tell Eden Dieters, "Eat a small portion (e.g. one serving) with satisfaction," rather than "Eat as much as you want until you're satisfied."

Jesus Fasted, *Feasted*, and Then Forgot About Food

When I first read the compulsive eating books back in college, I wasn't a Christian, and the self-serving undertones of the plan didn't really bother me. If anything, I liked the idea that I would get to indulge my desire for food so intensely each time I was hungry. I thought, "Why not please myself? I have nobody else to please."

After I became a Christian, however, my perspective changed. I even started wondering if it was displeasing to God or even sinful that I ate food with such intense satisfaction and pleasure. Did eating with pleasure constitute gluttony?

I read the Scripture on fasting and started thinking that perhaps it would be nobler to deprive myself as an offering to him rather than feed myself in his name. Jesus fasted for forty days, so I know that fasting can be a good thing to do.

But don't forget Jesus warned us to fast for the right reason, as a quiet act of worship to God, rather than to lose weight. Even a good thing can become bad if your attitude about it is wrong. You can fast with the right or wrong attitude just as you can eat with the right or wrong attitude.

For some reason, as I read through the Scriptures, I overlooked the passages that said Jesus feasted. Why? I suppose I was paying more attention to Satan and to the guilt I felt when I ate delicious food. Instead of believing the truth of God in the Book, I believed the liar when he told me I was fat and therefore I wasn't entitled to the same rights Jesus had to delicious food.

The Bible says Jesus came eating and drinking. He was called a glutton and a drunkard (Luke 7:33–35). But how could that be?

Wasn't Jesus perfect and sinless? Of course he was. His accusers were just twisting the truth because they were looking to find fault with him.

There is only one logical conclusion. If Jesus was indeed sinless, then to say that he feasted meant that he ate the right quantity of food for his body at the right time and for the right reason: for sustenance, fellowship, and praise to God. To say that he feasted certainly doesn't mean he pigged out.

Jesus could never be gluttonous. His feasting must have had more to do with his attitude rather than the choice or quantity or selection of food. To him feasting meant enjoying and celebrating during a meal and giving glory and thanks to God for the food and for the people with whom he ate.

When Jesus wasn't eating, he wasn't preoccupied with thoughts about food and eating, either. If anything, he told us to not worry about what we eat (Luke 12:29). He even told Martha to not worry about the food preparation when the big crowd was gathered at her house to hear him teach (Luke 10:38–42). And you know that crowd was going to be hungry soon.

When Jesus talked about food in between meals, it was only as a metaphor. He said, "I am the bread of life" (John 6:35), or he talked about it as a teaching tool so he could relate to those who were listening to him.

Nobody has been more perfect than Jesus when it comes to having the right attitude about food and eating. However, if you were to give out prizes for food asceticism, I think John the Baptist should win. John was known to fast often and abstain from wine, unlike Jesus, who came "eating and drinking."

John was so busy thinking about God that he ate locusts and wild honey just to shut up his hunger pangs. At least, I assume John ate the bugs for that reason. I suppose it's possible he just really enjoyed eating bugs.

If I were John, I would have dipped the locusts in the honey before eating them. On second thought, I would have skipped the entrée altogether and gone straight for the dessert.

I have a confession to make. The reason I'm digressing all of a sudden is that I'm procrastinating. I have to deal with a wrinkle in my reasoning. It's a wrinkle that irritates me as much in my real life as it does in my writing.

On one hand, I know I'm supposed to forget about food between meals, but on the other hand I have a family to feed and a busy schedule to juggle. It's unrealistic to completely forget about food in between meals unless you're a bug eater or unless you're like Jesus and can whip up a few thousand pounds of bread and fish in the blink of an eye.

Eventually my family expects food, just as the people at Martha's house were going to expect food. Therefore, I have to plan meals, shop for them, and cook them, not to mention clean up after them.

The only realistic solution is to simplify your life so you can think about food as little as possible, while at the same time finding a way to provide nutritious and delicious meals for your family. Plan your meals and grocery shop for an entire week (this hint is also commonly cited as a way to save money). Buy frozen dinners, rotisserie chicken, or prepared entrees. Make simple meals like tacos or chili or grilled cheese for dinner instead of pheasant under glass. Have breakfast foods for dinner. Grill meat on the weekend, and then reheat it for dinners during the week. When you cook, make double batches and freeze half. With a little practice and planning, you can focus more on the important things in life, as Mary was doing while Martha was cooking.

Be Like Children:
Nibble at Your Food and Play More

Even though childhood obesity is on the rise, in general, toddlers and very young children are less messed up when it comes to food than we grown-ups are. Therefore, I think we ought to look at some of their eating habits to figure out what they might be doing right. At least, we should look at the skinny children. This way we can see what we adults may be doing wrong.

First of all, when grown-ups aren't breathing down their necks to empty their plate, toddlers and preschoolers don't eat big meals. They nibble. They might eat a few bites, go play, come back to the table, eat a few more bites, and then go play more. They're picky eaters. They only eat what they like and have to be taught to eat and appreciate what they don't like, with repeated exposure to new foods. They play with their food and waste half of it, which annoys us grown-ups to no end. Of course, the minute the kitchen is clean and closed for the night, they want to eat again.

No matter how annoying their eating habits are to us grown-ups, let's face it: in some ways they're right and we're wrong. They're skinny and not in bondage, and we're fat and in bondage to food.

So copy your kids. Eat a small amount of food each time you're hungry, and leave the rest on the kitchen table. Look for a distraction elsewhere. Read Scripture, run errands, throw in a load of laundry, make a phone call, go for a walk, or pay some bills. Then go back to your plate twenty or more minutes later if you're still hungry. By that time, the nutrients will have hit your bloodstream, and the thought of eating the whole meal might just repulse you.

By prolonging your eating experience, you derive even more pleasure than if you ate your food all at once. Haven't you noticed that the first few bites are the best bites anyway? After that it's all downhill. Therefore, when you eat it in two separate sittings, fifteen or twenty minutes apart, you get to enjoy those exciting first bites twice instead of once.

In addition, young children don't think about food excessively between meals. They don't meticulously plan out their meals ahead of time, and they don't daydream about different recipes they want to try. They don't engage in conversations at the water cooler about eating or not eating, and they don't usually surf the Internet for websites about food.

They just respond to their bodies. Some days they eat a lot, probably because they are actively growing and feel hungrier than usual. Other days they couldn't care less about eating. Maybe they will want nothing but chicken strips and grapes one week and peanut butter and jelly sandwiches the next week. And they forget about food when they're not hungry.

Here again, my point is that children listen to their hunger pangs and their bodies more than internalized dogma regarding how to eat, and yet they manage to survive and grow.

Regarding what types of foods those young children choose to eat when they're hungry, that's where you, the grown-up, come in. You're the one who shops, so you're the one who controls what food gets into your house. You're in charge of influencing and shaping their attitudes based on the foods you expose them to (at least while they're young).

If you're worried that your children will want to eat cotton candy for breakfast, don't keep cotton candy in the house. Limit their access to junk food, and when they get hungry enough, they'll eat the grape tomatoes, baby carrots, and apples that you left in a bowl in the fridge.

But, here again, the main point is young children eat when they're hungry—and run around a lot when they're not.

In contrast, think about the habits and attitudes of most overweight adults. They are quite the opposite of children. They obsess about food, and they rarely play. Their playtime involves sedentary activities like sitting passively through dinner and a movie or watching a cooking marathon on the Food Network. Then they get fat, get sick, and die early. You tell me who has it right, the children or the adults.

Finally, as you emulate the eating habits of children (or thin adults), be careful you don't just see what you want to see. You might observe Junior eat like a horse some days. However, don't forget about the days when he eats like a bird. Just because you witness somebody eating a large meal, it doesn't mean they eat that way all the time. And Junior may have more lean body mass and may exercise more than you do.

God's Word told us that we must be fools to be wise, and that we should become like little children in regard to evil. I think that means we should get busy praying as well as playing, and we should "forget" to eat until our hunger pangs remind us.

Learn to Eat Small Portions of Food with Full Satisfaction

I've summarized what this chapter teaches in this chart so that you can refer back to it again and again as you practice eating mindfully. One warning about this exercise: I will explain in taste-bud-tantalizing detail how you should eat with enjoyment. Therefore, if you're not hungry now, skip this exercise and come back to it when you *are* hungry. Otherwise, ironically, I might tempt you to eat!

1. **Determine if you are truly physically hungry.** Differentiate your psychological or emotional cravings from the physical need to eat food. (If you need help with this, review the Apple Test on pages 90 – 92.)

2. **If you are truly hungry, decide what food you are hungry for.** Start to imagine how different foods will taste and feel in your mouth. Are you in the mood to crunch away on snack food? Or are you in the mood for some warm, soothing soup or hot chocolate? Do you want a sweet treat like ice cream? Or a hearty meal like chicken and dumplings? Try to determine the exact food that will satisfy you both physically and emotionally.

3. **Decide on the portion size.** Maybe you will take a "half" portion or less, compared to your previous portion size. Or maybe you will take one or two fist-size quantities of food, depending on the type of food and other factors, such as your degree of hunger, your lean body mass, your exercise level, and so on.

4. **Don't go back for seconds.** Instead of putting only a few slivers of food on your plate and then going back for another sliver every three minutes, take your entire portion of one or two fistfuls of food at once. Put it all on the plate so you can see it all together and get an honest assessment of how much you're eating. When you eat in a piecemeal manner, eating fourteen individual slivers of cake each time you pass through the kitchen, you underestimate your true

portion size. In addition, make sure you have enough to be able to leave at least one bite of every food on your plate.

5. **Create the right eating environment.** Just as you may have a special place in your home where you like to pray, designate a special place to eat, like at the kitchen table. Or maybe even at the "special" dining room table. Avoid eating in those places where you previously ate without thinking, for example, in the car, standing over the kitchen sink, at the counter, in front of the refrigerator, or while watching television. When you sit down to eat, light candles if you want to make your meal extra special. Tune out surrounding stimuli. Turn off the television and the radio.

6. **Remember the Provider of the food and pray.** For a moment, reflect on the wonder and the beauty of the food God gave you and then pray to him, either aloud or silently. Give him thanks not only for the food itself but also for the renewed attitude that allows you to feast on it without guilt. Ask him to help you know exactly when to stop eating, as well. Your prayer will also help you to become calm and focused.

7. **Eat with pleasure.** After you pray, go ahead and start eating. As you eat, *pay attention* to your meal. Don't rush your eating to get rid of the evidence, because you don't have to hide the fact you're eating, even if the food is fattening. You have as much right to good food as anyone else. Eat slowly and savor each morsel, drinking sips of water in between bites and thanking God for the freedom from bondage. Put your fork down in between bites. Concentrate on the taste and texture of the food in your mouth at that moment, and thank God for it as you eat.

8. **Take a break from eating.** By now, depending on the volume you ate, you might choose to stop eating for a while. Wrap the rest of your food and save it for the next time you feel real hunger pangs, if you even want it then. I hope you prolonged the eating experience as long as possible to optimize your satisfaction and to allow your stomach the greatest opportunity to register the food. You can always finish your meal the next time you're hungry.

continued on next page

9. **Stop eating when you feel the food in your stomach.** As soon as you barely begin to feel the food in your stomach, stop eating. At first, it may be difficult to judge when you feel this sensation because you may be out of touch with your internal signals. However, it's not the end of the world if you misjudge. If you undershoot and eat too little, it just means that you will become hungry again sooner rather than later. If you overshoot and eat too much, it will take longer before you become hungry again. Don't get bogged down in the technical details of how much to eat, or it will detract from your joy and satisfaction in eating. Get out of your head and get into your body!

10. **Thank God for the joy and satisfaction from the meal, and then move on to other thoughts.** When you are hungry again, acknowledge your hunger pangs, but allow yourself to become distracted until they grow to the point where you'd eat an apple (mild to moderate hunger). At that point, repeat the process of identifying what you want to eat and then feed your hunger again, just as God intended.

Show the Food Who Is Boss
by Not Eating All of It

At one time, when you were in bondage to food, you stopped eating when the food was gone. Food was the boss over you, and the only way you could control it was to eat it all up.

Now you understand Jesus is the Lord over you, and you are the boss over the food. Now your mission is to learn to leave food on your plate, even if it's only one bite, because when you leave food on your plate, you show it (and yourself and God) who is boss.

At first you may only be able to leave a few bites of food on your plate. That's okay. Every little bit helps. Besides, at first it's more about breaking the habit of eating for external reasons than it is about the calories. It's also about attuning to the hunger and satiety system God programmed into you, and about showing the food you have control over it, rather than vice versa.

When you leave food on your plate, you might worry that if you eat too little at this meal, you will be hungry again in too short a time. However, you shouldn't worry. If you do feel real hunger pangs again soon, you can eat again once they become moderate. That might be in only two hours, and if that's the case, it's okay. Eat again in two hours if you are hungry. It just means you are doing well listening to your body and you're eating small portions like you should.

If the quantity you eat seems small, don't second-guess your decision. Your current idea of what is "too little" is based on distorted worldly perceptions. Eventually your actions will affect your attitudes, and you will have a completely new idea of what should be "normal."

Besides, if you are at a restaurant, you can take the rest of the food home and eat it for your next meal. Thus, you're not really depriving yourself of the goodness; you're just delaying your gratification.

When you think of your decision to stop eating at the right time as an offering to God, you can understand that every little bite taken beyond the point of physical satiety is significant. Each bite you leave behind is yet another wonderful act of worship. The more you do it, the easier it gets. Before long, you will be able to leave much more food on your plate without hesitation, in a more reflexive and immediate offering to him.

Remember, part of your extrication from bondage is coming to the place where you no longer seek your pleasure and affirmation only from food. You obtain pleasure from pleasing God.

This practical advice works well for me: if I am in the middle of eating, and I receive a thought to "stop!" then I have to immediately stop eating. I try not to sit there and say, "Aw, come on, God; can't I have just one or two more bites?" If I do, I might second-guess what my inner voice told me and then continue eating. Instead, I swiftly put the fork down, get up, and wrap the rest for later.

Eat Mindfully

If you think you eat like a bird but can't lose weight, you may be eating more than you think.

Research shows most people underestimate the amount they eat, and this tendency is particularly strong among obese people.[1] If you were to actually measure your food, you might find that what you thought was a four-ounce pork chop was actually eight ounces, or what you thought was one cup of soup was actually two cups.

Another possibility is you may eat mindlessly, as Dr. Wansink points out in his book. You may just be unaware of the real amount of food you take in because you're distracted.

Eating mindlessly is a dangerous habit because if you are distracted when you eat, you can easily lose touch with your bodily sensations and eat too much. Adding insult to injury, when you don't pay attention, you don't get to fully feel satisfaction from the eating experience either. You gain weight without even getting to enjoy the food.

Do you eat mindlessly when you cook? Perhaps you adjust the seasoning so many times on the stew and mashed potatoes that you eat half a dinner just while you are cooking. Maybe you eat four cookie-dough balls as you scoop the dough onto the pan, somehow not counting the dough as having actual cookie calories. Then, after you are done cooking, and by the time you sit down with the family to eat, you're already half full. But you eat a full serving of stew and cookies out of a sense of obligation.

Then again, maybe it's not so much the average quantity of food you eat that's the problem, but more the pattern in which you consume it. Maybe you gained weight because you eat in an extreme way, alternating between overeating and undereating, which messed up your metabolism. Maybe you think you eat like a bird because you only remember the days when you eat like a parakeet and forget about the days when you eat like a raptor. A raptor is a bird too.

The Eden Diet is about exposing the lies about eating. If you believe you already eat like a bird and therefore it's not possible for you to lose weight, I want to liberate you from this mistaken belief. The real truth is probably that you eat mindlessly, you underestimate your portion sizes, you eat inconsistently, you don't exercise enough, you don't pay attention when you eat, you eat intermittently for emotional reasons, or you have some other habit that has caused you to gain weight.

Keeping a food diary can help you discover whether you eat mindlessly or if you have other habits that could sabotage your weight-loss efforts. However, keeping a food diary can be counterproductive. For example, if you are already losing weight on this plan, it probably means you are beginning to eat in a more natural way, according to your bodily signals. If this is the case, you should probably skip over this section. It would go against the whole premise of this plan, which is to become *less* preoccupied with food.

However, if you haven't lost as much weight as you wanted to, then keep reading.

Keeping a Food Diary

As you keep a food diary, be sure to have the right attitude about it. Instead of thinking of it as a way to police the way you eat, as if Big Brother were watching you, think of it as a tool God has given you so you can learn the truth. Instead of trying to be "extra good" when you keep the diary, try to let it reflect an average cross section of your eating. You have to be honest with yourself as well as with God if you want to move forward in your Romans 12:1–2 mental makeover.

Try to record your entries immediately after you eat the food, not at the end of the day. If you delay making the entry into the diary, you may forget the emotion or situation that triggered you to eat. In addition, you may remember your meals, but you may not remember the ten or twelve little tidbits you might have eaten mindlessly during the course of the day.

In addition, record specific details about what you eat. Instead of writing "casserole," write "one scoop of chicken enchilada casserole

Food Diary Sample Entry

Date: _____

	Why I ate:	Old Habit or New Habit?
Breakfast:		
3/4 cup oatmeal	Hungry	New: didn't eat every bite, didn't wolf it down, paid attention.
2 tsp. real butter		
1 T. brown sugar		
Water		
Lunch:		
Diet lemonade		
2 1/2 slices pepperoni pizza	Hungry, irritable	In between. I told myself I would only have one slice, but was distracted and got more. Stressful day.
Dinner:		
Chef salad with cheese,	Dinnertime	Old. Wasn't hungry; ate a big lunch.
turkey, veggies, croutons		Picked salad because not hungry.
Dressing		Should have just waited.
Diet pop		
Snacks:		
3 mini chocolate bars	Tired	Old. Should have rested.
Apple	Hungry	New. Enjoyed it.

Food Diary

Date: _____

| | *Why I ate:* | *Old Habit or New Habit?* |

Breakfast:

Lunch:

Dinner:

Snacks:

What I did right:

_____

_____

_____

Where did I consume calories that I might have otherwise not counted previously? What mindless eating habits did I discover?

_____

_____

_____

with corn, cheese, chilies, onions, and flour tortillas." It makes you really pay attention and embrace the little nuances of the food you're eating so that you can appreciate the food more.

As soon as you become more aware of your mindless eating habits, please stop keeping the diary. Normal eaters don't keep a food diary, and since your goal is to eat more normally, you don't have to either. It's just an exercise to help you recognize the fattening habits you may previously have been unaware of.

Conclusion

God made us to relish our food during meals but then to forget about it as much as possible in between meals. However, many people, especially chronic dieters, do the opposite. They eat in such a way that they do not experience joy during their meals, and then they obsess about food between meals.

That mind-set and those habits make us fat. If we want to get skinny, we need to get back to how God designed us in the beginning. We have to recapture the joy of eating during our meals by slowing down and by actually paying attention to the little nuances of what we eat. We should consider our meals to be gifts from God and realize that we are allowed to eat them without guilt, at the right time, and in the right amount.

The outcome of this method is amazing, really. Enjoying your food while you're eating it causes you to think about it less in between meals. Then, between meals, you can shift your attention off of food and back onto God, where it belongs.

The Eden Diet in Action

If food is your best friend,
it's also your worst enemy.
Edward "Grandpa" Jones, 1978

My husband had never seen me consume my own body weight in food until we vacationed at Epcot Center at Walt Disney World. As we ate lunch in "Norway," he realized that I had a hollow leg. We were newlyweds, and I had managed to keep my hollow leg a secret during our courtship.

I still remember his jaw dropping as I packed away plate after plate of smoked salmon from the buffet. To this day, I still don't understand how I did it—or why. It was like some kind of alien force took over my body and gave me superhuman salmon-consuming powers.

I'm still a little blurry on the details (probably because of the subsequent salmon-induced coma), but I suppose I did it because I was a poor student, the salmon was expensive and delicious, and it was a buffet.

Seemingly every other day, we engage in celebrations that involve food. If it isn't a birthday party, a bridal or baby shower, a wedding, an anniversary, or a graduation, then it's a Valentine's Day dinner date, an Easter dinner, a Mother's Day brunch, a Father's Day barbecue, a Fourth of July picnic, a Thanksgiving or Christmas dinner, or lunch in "Norway."

Or maybe it's a restaurant lunch or dinner, a vacation meal, a tailgate party, a movie date, an office party, a family reunion, a potluck at work or at church, or an after-school or after-work club activity or other social event that requires the mandatory eating of snacks.

Let's be honest with ourselves. Add up all those so-called "special events," and by the year's end, we can accrue seventy or eighty "just this once" social occasions to rationalize overeating.

Obviously, it's a bad idea to eat extra because it's a special occasion. If you overeat by only a few hundred calories at each event, you can easily gain five pounds by the end of the year. Multiply that by twenty years, and the sum total is the middle-aged washtub stomach that is associated with diabetes, heart disease, and other medical misery.

Because I don't want you to be overweight and sick, I'm going to give you specific strategies in this chapter so you can eat properly at all those "just this once" events. Not only will I help you to make better choices at the Thanksgiving dinner with the family, but also when you eat at restaurants, buffets, and potlucks.

You wouldn't go into a military battle without a strategy, would you? Then don't go into a buffet restaurant without a strategy. That's a kind of battle too.

Also in this chapter, I'll answer frequently asked questions about whether or not you should breakfast if you are not hungry, how to budget your food intake, how to get your hunger pangs in sync with your scheduled mealtimes, how to eat high-calorie treats in moderation, and how to eat on the Eden Diet if you are very obese or if you are ill.

Hopefully, these specific strategies will help you to lose weight and keep it off so that you can have the healthier body God intended for you in the beginning.

Food Volume Budgeting

Think of your food intake as though it were financial budgeting. In the same way that you might have only "X" number of dollars to last you the month, you can eat only a certain amount of food in a given day if you want to lose weight.

Believe it or not, many thin people budget their food intake. They might not be fully aware they do it, but they often reduce their food intake either before or after "splurges." Generally, they cut back on extras like dessert and snacks. They eat smaller portions, they stay hungry a little longer before eating, and they eat lower-calorie food, like fruits and vegetables. And if they see they've gained a few pounds, they cut back even more. If you don't believe me, just ask them.

Thin people even seem to budget their food within the meal. If their entrée is only so-so, and they really want dessert, they don't eat much of their entrée. You have heard it said, "Save room for dessert," right? That's what thin people do.

I've been told about a restaurant in Colorado that serves an extra-small entrée they call "The Good Excuse." That way their customers don't feel quite as guilty when they order the restaurant's famous desserts. Unfortunately, we don't have that restaurant where I live, so I had to come up with my own "Good Excuse." I order an appetizer instead of an entrée and then split it with a like-minded friend. Then we can even share dessert!

What If You Aren't Hungry for Breakfast?

Most successful long-term losers of weight make it a habit to eat breakfast, based on data in the National Weight Control Registry (NWCR, a database on the habits of people who have successfully maintained weight loss).[1] Even though I'm not registered with them, I meet their criteria. And I too eat breakfast nearly every day.

However, beware of how you interpret what I just said. I don't eat breakfast because somebody told me I should, because I'm trying to follow some optimal scientifically proven schedule, or because people in the database do it. I eat breakfast because I feel *hunger pangs* in the morning.

If you are eating less so you can lose weight or maintain the loss, then you should become hungry by mid to late morning, as well. If you don't, then you probably eat more food than you realize at other times of the day. For example, if you eat a big evening meal, it can keep you from feeling hungry the next morning. Or if you don't exercise enough, your metabolism might be sluggish, and your body might not have reason to demand food early in the morning.

If you're fixated on why you're not hungry the first thing in the morning, then shift your focus. Rather than overthink this issue, fine-tune your habits so that you *do* become hungry in the morning. Cut back further on your dinnertime portion size and/or exercise more so that your body will demand food the next morning.

Voila! Problem solved! Now you can eat breakfast according to your God-given hunger pangs, just as you're supposed to do at all the other times.

The only exception I can think of is if your job or school or other responsibilities preclude you from eating more flexibly, in response to your physical needs. If that's the case, then you might have to eat something small for breakfast before you leave the house, whether you're hungry or not. Otherwise, you might be absolutely famished by lunchtime and be tempted to overeat, and your metabolism might begin to shut down because your body thinks there's a famine.

If you're up for an experiment to test my advice, try this: take a survey of the eating habits of obese versus thin people. Ask them if they eat breakfast when they're not hungry. I can almost guarantee that most of your thin friends will act embarrassed and say apologetically, "I know I'm supposed to eat breakfast, but I just don't feel hungry then." Your heavy friends, on the other hand, will proudly say, "Of course. If I don't eat breakfast, my metabolism will shut down."

Okay, let's pull the camera back and use a little common sense here. Which group is thinner, the one that eats according to dogma or the one that eats according to hunger pangs? Don't you think that's suspicious? If eating breakfast when you're not hungry were the right choice, then your fat friends would be thin and your thin friends would be fat.

It makes me wonder if we aren't just coming up with excuses to eat when we're not hungry, just because we like to eat. Ouch! Sometimes the truth hurts, doesn't it?

No matter what evidence the researchers offer, I can't believe that worldly wisdom could be smarter than God working in you. Only God knows exactly what your body needs at any given time, and his compass within you is hunger. So forget about dogma, trust God working in you, and eat breakfast when and if you're hungry for it.

What If You Aren't Hungry at the Same Time as Everyone Else?

When you begin to eat in response to hunger, you might feel hungry at odd times that don't coincide with everyone else's idea of what is normal. In this case, you might have to fiddle a little bit with your eating pattern so your body becomes hungry around the times when other people usually eat. That way you can still enjoy meals with the rest of civilization.

Here's a simple strategy that should help. If you become hungry a couple hours before your scheduled eating appointment (e.g., dinner with the family), then eat a *tiny* snack that will tide you over until dinner. You can probably get by eating an apple, a slice of bread, one cookie, or something else that's small.

On the other hand, if it's three or four hours before your eating engagement, then you might need to eat a little more, like half a sandwich, so that you're not absolutely famished by the time you sit down to eat with everybody else. You see, there's no law that says you have to eat a full meal every time you're hungry.

Remember, becoming hungry is not an emergency. You're a mature adult, not a baby. You can delay gratification and eat only a tiny snack to tide you over until your meal with others. (Of course, if you're diabetic or sick in some other way, you should disregard what I say and do what your doctor tells you.)

If your family or friends normally eat together at scheduled times, your new habits might rock the boat a little. They might expect you to eat with them and in large quantities, regardless of how your stomach feels. Perhaps that's just how it was with them in the past, and they're resistant to change.

If this is the case, explain that you need their support even if they don't understand or agree with you. Then reassure them you will do your best to join them for meals as soon as you get your hunger pangs to coincide with theirs. Just don't be surprised if they say, "What are hunger pangs?"

How to Eat Backward Dinner

If you have a sweet tooth like I do, you might sometimes look forward to dessert more than you look forward to the actual entrée. Maybe you have the opportunity to eat a particularly delicious dessert you have been craving. If that's the case, why not make the special dessert your whole meal instead of eating it after an entrée?

That's right, you heard me: your whole meal can be a piece of pie.

I know it sounds like nutritional blasphemy, but let's face facts. By the time you finish your entrée, you're usually not hungry for dessert, anyway. You just eat it because it looks and tastes good, and consequently, you take in calories your body doesn't need.

Don't get me wrong, I'm not advocating you eat dessert for dinner all the time. If you did, you might get sick. I am only saying that, every now and then, and depending on the circumstances (like your general state of health), it may be okay or even good for you to eat a special treat as your entire meal.

My skinny friend Tammy calls it "backward dinner." That's where you eat dessert first, and then you go back and eat some of the entrée if you're still hungry. If Tammy can do it occasionally and stay healthy and slim, then you and I should be able to as well. Who knows? Maybe an occasional backward dinner is even why she's slim.

How to Eat to the Glory of God at Buffets and Potlucks

A friend of mine once said, "If you walk into a restaurant and see a lot of overweight people, run!" This is great advice. Unfortunately, this means you'll probably have to run away from any buffet restaurant you walk into. Overweight people are attracted to buffets like moths to a flame.

The reason is obvious. Buffets appeal to our gluttonous and greedy sin nature. Something deep within us makes us stuff ourselves with delicious food and then rationalize that we ate to get our money's worth.

I'd like to take a minute right now to clear up any confusion: Paul told us to "buffet" (verb, pronounced "buff-it") our bodies in 1 Corinthians 9:27 (AMP). He didn't say to "buff-aye" our bodies (e.g., with smoked salmon, like I did at Epcot).

The two meanings are opposite. To buffet ("buff-it") one's body is a good thing. It means to toughen it up through painful self-discipline, like a boxer might do to train for a fight. The other kind of buffet (as in "all-you-can-eat") can be a bad thing for the body. The overabundance of food leads to our softening and weakening and opens the door to disease.

Learn to think about buffets the way thin people do. Thin people are conscious of their money too. They know that if they go to a buffet, they will leave either feeling ripped off because they didn't eat enough to justify the cost, or they will overeat and leave feeling bloated and sick. So they don't go very often, and neither should you if you have any choice in the matter.

But what if you don't have a choice? Let's say, for the sake of discussion, that you're forced to eat at a buffet. Maybe you're on a trip and it's the only type of restaurant available. Or maybe your group picked it without your vote. In those cases, you're going to need a strategy for damage control. You need to be able to come out of the buffet victorious, having demonstrated you control the food rather than vice versa.

This is how to be victorious when you eat at buffets: first, notice how you feel when you walk into the restaurant. Because of the frenzy at the buffet line, it's not unusual to feel panicked or afraid, as though you have to get your share before the food is all gone. Of course, the danger in feeling panicked or competitive over the food is that you might be inclined to take more food than you actually need.

Just remember Yoda's immortal words in the Star Wars movies, "Fear is the path to the dark side." You must lose your fear if you are to conquer the buffet.

To conquer your fear, quote Scripture and pray. It will help you to relax and focus. Thank *Jesus* for being Lord of your life, and tell him you know the food is not lord over you. Also remember your God is one of abundance. This means there should be plenty of food for you, even if you are the last in line.

Not only should you remember Jesus is the Lord over the food, you should also remember he is the Lord over the facility in which you are eating, and he is the Lord over you and the people you are eating with, whether they know it or not.

When you go to the line, you might even rebuke the food (under your breath). Say, *"Jesus is Lord*, and you are not." I know it sounds crazy, but this approach has worked for me in all kinds of situations. It demotes the food from having any kind of power over me and realigns my thinking with the truth: because of my association with Jesus Christ, I have control over the food rather than vice versa.

As you get ready to choose your food, I would recommend surveying the entire buffet, including breads, salads, and desserts, before you put any food on your plate. Then you'll know which food you want the most, and you won't fill your plate with things you don't want and then at the end see something else you want more—and be tempted to eat all of it.

Try to put a small serving of the food you want the most on your plate first, even if it's dessert. If you want to try two or three desserts, take a sliver of each, with the total amount equaling one small portion. (Remember that a portion is probably only half of what you think it is!)

After you choose your favorite food, then go to your next favorite, and so forth, until you have put a volume of one or two fistfuls of food on your plate.

In addition, I recommend that you put all your food on one plate, including the bread, salad, entrees, side dishes, and dessert, if you want those. If you want soup, then put the cup or bowl on the plate too, and put your other food around it. Obviously, if you decide to eat all of those categories of foods, your portion sizes of each will have to be very tiny to all fit on the plate.

Try to select only a few of the foods you absolutely love, or foods that are unique or different or that you rarely get to have. Don't waste the precious space on your plate by putting bread or salad or other common food on it if more special food is available.

Some slim people I know avoid temptation by bringing food they don't particularly like to potluck buffets. For example, if you love chocolate chip cookies but you don't care either way about oatmeal cookies, then make oatmeal cookies for the function you're attending. Hey, somebody there will eat them. And if not, you won't be overly tempted to eat the leftover food.

I do a similar thing regarding the candy I buy for Halloween. I buy candy I don't care for. That way, if some candy is left over, I don't feel particularly inclined to eat it.

Be choosy about your selections because you have a food-volume budget. It doesn't make sense to eat food that is only so-so or common when you have the opportunity to eat foods that are particularly special or interesting. What law said you have to eat a little bit of every common food on the buffet just because it's there?

Regarding the total volume of the food you select, remember that the size of your empty stomach is about the size of your fist. If you take double that amount in food, you should have more than enough to eat to your satisfaction and leave at least one or two bites of everything on your plate. (Knowing that you have to leave a bite or two of everything forces you to pay closer attention. It helps you to avoid cleaning your plate mindlessly.)

As you eat, take sips of water between bites. This will enhance the flavor of each individual bite by clearing your palate, and it will also help you feel more satisfied by a smaller volume of food. It also has the effect of slowing your rate of eating so that you have time to enjoy what you're eating and to reach satiety.

If you try one of the foods on your plate and you think it's just okay, don't take another bite of it. Instead, try the next item on your plate. If it's great, eat it. If it's just okay, skip it and try the next item.

If none of your selections are great, but you like the dessert, then eat nearly the whole dessert. Eat it first if you want to. Once you begin to feel full, you will find it easier to leave boring food on your plate rather than delicious food.

As you eat, make a conscious effort to tune out the sights and sounds and the chaos all around you. Tune in to the sensory experience of eating the food on your plate, and tune in to an attitude of praise and thanksgiving to God for the food.

If you are eating and talking with other people, stop eating while you're talking. When you're not in conversation, go back to concentrating on the food. Otherwise, you might become distracted and miss the onset of your fullness signals.

Don't rationalize that you'll eat less at a later meal if you eat more at this one, because it's probably not true. In a study by B. J. Rolls, subjects who were given potato chip snacks didn't make up for the added calories by eating less at their subsequent meal.[2]

You're better off trying to undereat in the meals leading up to your restaurant meal. Or if you haven't done that and you end up overeating, pray for the discipline to cut back in a few meals afterward.

You will have plenty more opportunities to eat at buffets in your lifetime, so you don't have to eat it all now. Remind yourself if you are eating at a restaurant buffet that you can go back to the restaurant anytime you want to and have more of any particular food you liked.

Romans 12:2 tells you to "not conform to the pattern of this world." In this scenario, that means you shouldn't use the people around you as your plumb line. Just because someone else has four empty plates piled on the corner of the table at the buffet restaurant doesn't mean you have to copy their bad habits. Remember, gluttony is a sin (Proverbs 23:2).

Instead, use God's plumb line, the one he programmed into you. Eat only when you feel hunger pangs, and eat in much smaller portions than the world would have you believe is normal.

How to Deal with People or Situations That Trigger You to Overeat

Perhaps you have mixed feelings about eating with certain people or going to certain places that you once associated with overeating. Believe me, I can relate. On the one hand, I enjoy returning to New York to see my family, but on the other hand, it makes me nervous to return to the environment where I used to pig out on large quantities of food.

Ironically, everyone in my family is slim now, and we don't dwell on food the way we did many years ago. But I still carry around baggage that makes me feel nervous when I go there. So far God hasn't shown me how to get over that, but maybe it's because I haven't asked.

If you have to return to a place where you might feel the urge to overeat, try to remember that the food doesn't have any control over you except for what *you* give it. Food is not lord over you; *Jesus* is. No food actually jumps into your mouth and forces you to eat it (unless maybe you're talking about veal saltimbocca, which in Italian literally means "veal that jumps into your mouth"). You have to decide to put food in your mouth, which means you can decide to not put it there too.

If the people you are visiting with have a dysfunctional attitude about food, you'll probably meet with extra resistance. Here is what I suggest: don't tell them you're on a reducing diet. Just start eating smaller portions of normal food and only when you're hungry. Eventually, you'll lose enough weight for them to notice, and then your methods will be more convincing.

When you're eating with others and are following this plan, I can almost guarantee that somebody will say, "Is that all you're going to eat?" Now, if you were a feisty person like I occasionally am, you could always gesture to their plate, saying, "Yes. Are you going to eat all that?" (Oops, that was my evil twin talking. Please don't really say that.)

Seriously, get ready to hear this: "Is that all you're going to eat?" The key is to prepare an answer ahead of time. Say, "I am saving room for dessert," "I'm just pacing myself," "I would rather eat less and not feel bloated," "I'm not very hungry right now," or "I'm going to be eating again in a little while, thanks."

Then change the subject and take the focus off of you. You might say, "I'm reading an interesting book called *The Eden Diet*. It has shown me that it isn't healthy to eat as much as I ate in the past. Since I've started eating smaller portions of food I enjoy, I feel so much better and I'm losing weight!"

If they persist at trying to get you to eat unnecessarily, ask them in a very polite, loving, and concerned way, "I can't help but wonder … why is it so important to *you* that I eat when I'm not hungry?" Of course, you (and they) already know the answer to that question. They probably want you to eat more so they don't feel as bad about how much they're eating. Misery and overeating loves company.

Please note that it's important to deal with criticism in the right way. Express your concern for those who give you unsolicited advice, rather than being defensive or offensive. If they cause you to feel angry, stop and pray for them for a few seconds in your mind before you respond. That way your words may come out in a more acceptable way, and maybe you can even help them improve their own eating habits.

How to Eat at Family Gatherings and on Holidays

Let's say it's Thanksgiving, and you're headed to Aunt Mabel's for dinner. As this is a fantasy exercise, I'll ask you to pretend that you actually like Aunt Mabel and that you actually want to be there. Also, pretend that your family members aren't crazy and that they don't stress you out and cause you to overeat or bore you and cause you to eat to avoid small talk. In other words, in this make-believe example, pretend you have a totally normal family and no emotional triggers that complicate the way you eat. The reason is, for now, I want to focus only on the technical issues of eating in buffet situations. Later on, we'll talk more about the emotional triggers caused by your crazy family.

For the sake of the example, assume that you have spent other holidays with the family, and you know who is known for what special dish. You probably already know which of those dishes you like and which you find boring or bland.

In this case, let's say the dish you have been most looking forward to is Aunt Mabel's pecan pie. Only, in past years, you always felt guilty when you ate it because you were usually already stuffed to the gills by the time dessert came around.

Here's an earth-shattering idea: tell Aunt Mabel you have been waiting for it all year, and ask her if you can eat a little bit of it before your entrée, when you're at the peak of your hunger pangs. Make it the first thing you put on your plate if it's the thing you want the most. She might think it's odd, but she'll be flattered too, I'd imagine.

Then, according to the advice I gave previously about how to eat at buffets, fill your plate with a little bit of whatever else looks good to you, taking enough to satisfy you, and knowing you won't be going back for seconds until the second wave of eating begins many hours later.

As usual, put all your food on one plate, including the dessert, the entrée, the side dishes, and whatever else you decide to eat. Also as usual, skip the dishes you get to eat all the time if there are more appealing choices available. Don't feel pressured to try everything just because it's there. Relax and pray for God's guidance to know when to stop eating, and then eat to the glory of God.

This is where the situation is slightly better than when you are at a restaurant buffet. Here, you're at someone's house. Assuming that the arrangement is informal and people are scattered throughout the house, you can take a rest break from eating so you can better pace yourself to ensure you don't overeat.

For example, after a few bites of the pecan pie, get up and pass out napkins, refill drinks, become engrossed in conversation, or take a restroom break. Try to find a reason to get up from your seat yet still be part of the holiday meal.

In the meantime, since the pecan pie has 10 million grams of sugar in it, the sugar will hit your bloodstream pretty fast to signal you to stop eating. If you delay the rest of your eating, the pie will act as an instant appetite suppressant, so you won't even want to eat much more when you return to the table.

After a short while, go back to your seat and take a few bites of the entrée and the side dishes, and decide if they are worth the calories. Is the Thanksgiving turkey just okay or is it great? If it's not great, but the pie is, slip the turkey to the dog under the table and eat more pie! It's not like you haven't eaten turkey before or you won't ever get it again. Otherwise, you'll eat the marginally satisfying turkey out of obligation and still eat the pie, when all you really wanted was the pie.

How to Eat Fast Food to the Glory of God

Let's say you're hungry for fast food but don't know what. Maybe you're thinking about a burger from your favorite greasy spoon or the gyros from the food court at the mall.

Take my advice: if you don't know what you want to eat, then don't even consider walking into the den of iniquity—oops! I mean the fast-food restaurant. Wait until you know for sure what you want, and then walk in. Otherwise, when you see and smell the food, you'll convince yourself that you were hungrier than you realized. Then you'll order too much.

Once you decide what you want and walk up to the counter to order, keep your eyes focused straight ahead on the cashier, not on the menu, breathe through your mouth so you don't smell the food, and order from memory. I'm telling you, when you walk into a fast-food restaurant, you're walking into enemy territory, so you have to be as clever as the enemy is.

Here is another way to be clever: forget about the combo meals and order à la carte. Order only one thing—either the burger or the fries, but not both. Or get a kid's meal. Sadly, it has enough food for an adult anyway.

Alternatively, if you order the combo, ask for a plastic knife and split the burger down the middle. Share half of the burger and half of the fries with a friend. I'd say to wrap half of it and eat it later, but, personally, I think leftover fast food is gnarly.

Finally, get ready for the cashier to say, "But the combo meal is a better deal than ordering à la carte." Okay, now think this through. Just because it's the best deal moneywise doesn't mean it's good for you to eat it.

Do you really think these people have your best interests in mind? Or do they just want your money and your repeat business? Hello! They aren't doing you any favors by trying to feed you more. No matter what the cashier is trained to say, and no matter how much he seems like he is trying to help you, the restaurant is in it for the profits. They are there to capitalize off you.

Don't let them. Order based on what you know to be true: God never intended for you to eat the large portions served in fast-food restaurants, anyway.

Beware of Portion Distortion!

There are pros and cons to eating à la carte. As previously mentioned, it's easier than eating at a buffet because you're limited to fewer choices. However, you can still easily eat too much, mostly because restaurant portions are so huge.

Going out for steak almost guarantees that the smallest cut available will be an eight ounce filet. Eight ounces is double what an average adult man needs to eat in protein at one meal. The smaller rib eye steak, weighing in at twelve ounces instead of sixteen, is called a "cowgirl cut" in one restaurant I know of, probably to embarrass the men into ordering the bigger cut.

In addition, many restaurants provide freebie incentives that come before the entrée, like chips and salsa, tortillas, or fresh-baked, all-you-can-eat bread. Then you get your full-sized salad with high-fat dressing. By the time your oversized entrée is served, you're already full.

It doesn't help that your oversized entrée comes on a fourteen-inch plate, either. Research proves that you eat more when you're served larger-sized restaurant portions.[3]

A study by Dr. David Levitsky, my old mentor at Cornell, showed that when young adults were served larger portions, they ate 39 percent more food than when they were served smaller portions. In other words, they tended to eat as much as was put in front of them.[4]

I maintain that it's now professional peer pressure for a chain restaurant to serve too much. It's either that or be driven out of business. If you found a restaurant that served sizes that were actually healthy and right, people would complain that the restaurant next door served twice as much for the same cost.

Portion sizes have even increased in the fast-food restaurants. Research shows that between 1977 and 1996, there was a forty-nine–calorie increase in a portion of soft drinks, a ninety-seven–calorie increase in a hamburger portion, and a sixty-eight–calorie increase in a portion of french fries, all because the size of the portion increased. If you ate all three of those things at one meal, which you typically do when you order a combo meal, then you would eat 214 more calories than you might have eaten in a similar meal in 1977.[5]

By my calculations, if you overate by that much every day for a year, you would gain twenty pounds of fat by the end of the year. It makes me want to shout, "Stop trying to supersize me!" I suppose that's why eating out was implicated as a major contributor to obesity by a recent Food and Drug Administration report.[6]

Should it be a surprise that there is a correlation between when portion sizes started to increase and when our weight started to increase? According to a study published in 2002, portion sizes started increasing in the 1970s, rose sharply in the 1980s, and have basically paralleled our increase in body weight over recent years.[7]

Here is my advice if you eat at à la carte restaurants. Depending on how much you like the freebie, go ahead and eat some. However, if you do, then when the entrée comes, take only one or two bites of it and box up the rest for your next day's lunch.

On the other hand, if you already know that you're going to like the entrée more than the freebie, then eat only a tiny bit of the freebie and the salad, and then eat half of the entrée. If you go light on the early courses, you might even be able to budget a few bites of dessert into your meal.

You can also eat less in the few meals leading up to that special outing and/or eat less in the meals afterward (however, you're less likely to follow through afterward, I'm afraid).

Even if you don't eat much of the freebie, you might consider asking for a to-go box anyway the moment you place your order. When your food comes, divide your entrée into two or three meals, and immediately put the remainder into the box for your lunches in subsequent days.

You could also practice your new normal eating skills by asking a like-minded friend to share the entrée with you. Consider it to be an opportunity to focus more on your friend than the food, just as Jesus would have done. Eat slowly and to the glory of God, and share not only the meal but also the information you learned from this book.

Can you still lose weight if you eat out? Of course! That's the beauty of the Eden Diet: you get to eat what you want. Remember, it's all about calories in and calories out. You might eat 800 calories at your restaurant lunch. However, you will feel so satisfied by the experience that you will probably be satisfied with a 300-calorie bowl of cereal or a sandwich for dinner. Throw in some exercise before your 200-calorie breakfast, and you still have a sizeable calorie deficit for the day!

How to Eat on the Eden Diet
If You Are Ill

If you are ill, check with your doctor regarding which foods you can continue to eat, and which, for health reasons, you have to give up.
As Paul said:

> "Everything is permissible for me"—but not everything is beneficial. "Everything is permissible for me"—but I will not be mastered by anything. "Food for the stomach and the stomach for food"—but God will destroy them both.
> 1 CORINTHIANS 6:12–13 NIV

In other words, depending on your situation, it may not be a good idea to eat junk food or backward dinner just because there is no biblical law against it.

If you have diabetes and you splurge on sugar, then you might go into a diabetic coma and die. If you have coronary artery disease and you eat high-cholesterol foods like eggs, you might have another heart attack. If you have high blood pressure and you eat salty foods like popcorn, you might have a stroke.

Your choices have consequences, so use your common sense and modify the Eden Diet as your health requires.

How to Eat to the Glory of God
If You're Extremely Overweight

Regardless of how much you weigh at the outset, the system is always the same. It doesn't matter if you're ten pounds overweight or if you're three hundred pounds overweight. Just wait until you feel hungry before you eat, eat small portions of any food you enjoy, and eat to the glory of God.

The main difference is that if you are morbidly obese, it will take you longer to reach your goal weight. But who cares? God willing, if you're still alive in two years, you'll be two years older no matter what you eat during that time. You might as well eat small portions of what you enjoy and lose weight slowly and steadily. It's just like the story of the Tortoise and the Hare; sometimes "slow and steady" wins the race.

If you are considerably overweight and you have not been able to follow any diet whatsoever, not even this one, you might also consider weight-loss surgery. Why? The answer is that God is merciful and sometimes works through bariatric surgeons to save your life.

If you decide to go the surgical route, however, be sure you understand the risks. In my opinion, weight-loss surgery should be considered only in the most extreme cases. For one thing, there are significant risks to any major abdominal surgery. For another, it's not a guaranteed solution to your problem. You can regain substantial amounts of weight in spite of the surgery if you continue to eat for external reasons afterward.

Even after weight-loss surgery, you still have to eat less and according to hunger if you want to keep the weight off. So you might want to commit to those habits now and avoid the surgery if possible.

Conclusion

As you put the Eden Diet into practice, you will probably find that different eating situations call for different strategies to optimize your chances of success. In this chapter, I offered you a variety of strategies I've had success with over the past twenty-five years. If you apply them, you should have an easier time eating according to hunger pangs in the majority of real-life social eating situations.

Part Three

How to Beat Temptation

Feed Emotional Hunger
the Right Way

If hunger is not the problem,
then eating is not the solution.
Author unknown

What do you think of when you hear the phrase "comfort food"? I think of the fresh, homemade tomato sauce my mom made when I was a kid. Every summer we went to a farm near our home and hand-picked bushels of roma tomatoes. After we sliced and simmered the tomatoes, we extracted the bright red puree and canned it in Mason jars for the winter. Throughout the year, my mom used that puree to make the best tomato sauce you ever tasted. On special occasions, she even added homemade Italian sausage to it and served it over pasta that she also made from scratch.

Most people are jealous when I tell them that story. All they can think about is how great it must have been to have a mom who could cook so well. Well, it *was* great—except for the fact that I abused the privilege. Instead of eating small portions of her delicious food and only when I was hungry, I ate too much of it and for all the wrong reasons, including for emotional reasons.

Take it from me: if you eat to find emotional consolation, it backfires. You become a bottomless pit for food, you gain weight, and you never actually find long-term emotional relief. You only become more miserable. I suppose that's why in the Scriptures, Paul said, "Food for the stomach and the stomach for food" (1 Corinthians 6:13), rather than, "Food is for filling your empty emotional spaces."

Thankfully, in my adult life, God blessed me with knowledge that allowed me to unlearn the habit of eating for emotional reasons. In this chapter I'll pass this knowledge on to you. That way you can get back to eating in response to hunger, which is what God intended in the beginning.

First I will reveal to you the roots of the emotions that mislead you to into eating when you're not hungry. In some cases, the root will be the desire to feel you are in control, when the truth is that only God is in control. In other cases, the root will be distorted beliefs and misperceptions that promote self-condemnation and depression. In still other cases, the root will be the idea you're deficient or missing something that somebody else has. In all cases, those beliefs manipulate you through your emotions to eat when you really need something else.

After I help you find the roots of your negative emotions, I will show you how to defuse their power over you with right thinking: the truth as God revealed it in the Bible. You will see that negative emotions lose their control over you when your thinking is aligned with Scripture. Right thinking leads you to make better choices, and that, in turn, allows you to disassociate your emotional triggers from the learned response of eating.

I want to give you a word of caution, though. If you are of the male persuasion, then you might find this chapter a little tedious to read. For you, reading about emotions is probably as much fun as going to the dentist or going shopping with your wife. But you should do it anyway. It's for your own good.

Men have emotions just as women do, even if they are less aware of them or don't want to be as aware of them. If you go on denying your emotions, you'll go on being controlled and manipulated by them, and it will be harder for you to lose weight. That's true even if the emotion is as straightforward as boredom, which is the number one reason men claim to eat when they're not hungry.

So before you have that obesity-induced heart attack and have to beg God for mercy on your deathbed, please accept my advice. Prayerfully explore the root of the emotions that affect the way you eat, and allow God to rectify your thinking so that you eat only when you're actually hungry.

The Emotional Eating Cycle

People who eat for emotional reasons generally do so in the evening, in the safety of their own home, and when they are alone. After the dust settles from the activities of the day, their suppressed negative emotions have a chance to surface. In turn, those negative emotions trigger them to eat as an escape. That way they don't have to experience those emotions directly. It's a psychological defense mechanism.

Sometimes, emotional eaters' food choices reflect the emotions they are trying to escape from. If they feel stress, anger, frustration, or anxiety, they might feel compelled to eat crunchy foods like popcorn, chips, or nuts, so they can nervously chomp away at their tension. If they feel depressed, they might be drawn to rich, creamy, or sweet foods to smooth away their bad feelings.

If they binge, they may consume many thousands of calories over a very short time. They might even "dissociate," or "zone out," which means they are wide awake but not fully aware of what they are doing. The mental departure serves as a means to experience less guilt while they are eating large volumes of food, and it also further separates them from their unwanted emotions.

Bingeing provides only a temporary vacation from the negative emotions that led them to overeat in the first place. Eventually their emotions come back, along with additional guilt and shame that result from the binge. Those emotions, in turn, lead to more emotional eating and more guilt and shame. It's a miserable, vicious cycle.

Why Do You Associate Food
with Emotions?

Do you wonder how you learned to associate food with emotional comfort? It probably started when you were a tiny little baby, while you were being fed in the comfort and security of your mother's warm, loving embrace. At least, that's a bonding experience I hope you were blessed to have.

The problem is, as you grew up, not all of the other messages that you learned about food and emotions were good for you. Some of them were downright wrong and harmful, like the message I learned one day when I was three years old.

I wasn't sure why I had to be at the pediatrician's office that day. I wasn't sick. All I knew is that there were two nurses, one on each side of me, and for some reason, each one was gripping one of my earlobes with a cold, silver, metal thing. Suddenly and in unison, they squeezed the silver things, and then I felt sharp, sticking pains shoot through both earlobes. Not only did it confuse me and cause me physical pain, it also frightened me. So, understandably, I started crying.

Without skipping a beat, one of the nurses literally shoved a lollipop into my mouth, which, in turn, confused me further. I remember thinking, "Huh? Why did that mean lady force a lollipop into my mouth? My ears hurt. Wait a minute ... Mmmm. Grape! ... Mmmm ... Now, what was I crying about again?"

In hindsight, I realize the nurse who shoved the lollipop into my mouth probably wanted to help me feel better. But I wonder if she did it in part to help herself feel better. Who knows? Maybe she felt guilty on an unconscious level for hurting me. The sooner she could distract me with food, the sooner she could stop feeling bad about impaling me with earrings against my will.

Now that I'm a parent, I understand how it works. Sometimes we're tempted to pacify our kids with food, or with television, or with cell phones, or with anything it takes to stop their crying and whining. We rationalize that it's to "cheer them up" or "calm them down," but, in a way, it makes *us* feel better too. When our kids are happy, we parents are happy.

I'm not saying that it's a crime to give your toddlers a cookie while you grocery shop with them, but if you do it when they're not hungry so *your* shopping trip is a happier experience, then you become part of the problem. You're just teaching your child to use food to distract themselves from boredom and fatigue. It's the same as when you cheer them up with ice cream because they fell and scraped their knee. You're teaching them to eat to avoid negative emotions.

Do you remember the research Pavlov did with dogs, where he fed them right after ringing a bell? Eventually the dogs started to salivate when they heard the bell because they associated eating with hearing the bell ring.

It turns out that we're just like Pavlov's dogs. Growing up, we were taught by various means to reflexively eat when we felt unwanted emotions, whether or not we were hungry. Just like the dogs, we have a conditioned response.

In a way that's actually great news. If we have been conditioned to seek food when we feel negative emotions or when we need comfort, then we can be deconditioned; we can unlearn that behavior. That's what I hope to help you do in this chapter, with the assistance of the Holy Spirit.

Stress

I recall a phenomenon my mentor at Cornell taught me about: if you stress rats by putting a painful clip on their tail, they increase certain activities like eating.

I don't know about you, but I can relate to those critters. Particularly when I was in college and medical school, I recall numerous instances when I ate to get my mind off of the academic stress on my tail.

The rat experiment suggests to me that the cure for stress eating is to take off the clip. Find a way to lose some of your unnecessary burdens. Determine the root of your stress and defuse it at its source. For example, if you eat because your finances stress you out, then stop spending more than you earn. Seek God's plan for getting out of debt. Try Dave Ramsey's Financial Peace University program available through most churches.

On the other hand, if the root of your stress is your overly full schedule, then declutter your life. Get rid of activities not ordained by God, and retain activities necessary to maintain your health and fulfill your purpose in his kingdom. If you'd like a reference for time management, read *Tyranny of the Urgent* or *Freedom from Tyranny of the Urgent*, both by author Charles E. Hummel. For additional advice regarding time management for weight loss, refer to Appendix B.

Alternatively, if your stress is rooted in sin, then confess it to God, forsake it, and accept his complete and total forgiveness. You have nothing to lose. He already knows about your sin whether you confess it or not.

I think you get my point. You have to look for the root of your stress and then defuse the emotion by correcting the actual cause, when possible.

If you have trouble processing and getting to the root of your stress, then you might need to temporarily redirect it. Get away from the stressful situation, and also get away from the food. Get some exercise. Go for a bike ride. Turn on the radio and dance and sing to the glory of God. If you've already exercised for the day, then relax to the audio recording "Godly Affirmations for Weight Loss" (available on www.TheEdenDiet.com), or listen to some soothing music.

If those options aren't practical at the time you feel stressed, then click a pen, tap your feet, or squeeze a stress ball.

Ultimately, though, distracting yourself and redirecting your stress are only short-term ways to deal with it. Eventually you have to learn to let go of it altogether, as Jesus did. He felt stressed at times too, like when he was in the garden at Gethsemane, anticipating a brutal, torturous death as well as a temporary pit stop in hell (John 12:27). Uh-huh. That would certainly stress me out a tad bit.

What did Jesus do when he was in stressful situations? He certainly didn't stress-eat. He trusted in God. I know that because he counseled others in the same way. He said, "Do not let your hearts be troubled. Trust in God; trust also in me" (John 14:1).

In essence, Jesus said that you have a choice regarding how you think about and respond to stress. In the midst of a stressful situation, you may *choose* to feel stressed out, or you may choose to trust in God. Obviously, it's for your own good to choose the latter.

Jesus also prayed to deal with stress, and you obviously should too. When you pray, ask God for discernment: "Lord, what is really stressing me out here? Am I seeing the real truth in the situation, or is my perception clouded with lies? Should I try to change the situation or just adjust my perception of it? By the way, why am I afraid to just sit still and feel stress? Why do I feel the need to distract myself from the emotion by eating? What would happen if I just experienced stress without eating in response to it?"

In summary, the way to handle stress is to minimize the root of your stress, redirect your urge to eat by choosing physical exercise, and, most importantly, pray for revelations and trust in God. If you do those things, you will feel less stressed, and therefore you'll feel less compelled to stress-eat.

Frustration

I experienced frustration occasionally during college and medical school. If there was a concept I had trouble understanding or a task I had trouble accomplishing, I became frustrated and I ate.

Later in life I learned that frustration is due to an inability to control. That's when the light bulb went on over my head and I began to understand the root of my stress-eating behavior. It turned out that when I felt that I couldn't control myself, the people around me, or my situation, I reached out for something I could control, like food.

Eating might have distracted me for a while from my situation, but it didn't give me more control over it. After I finished eating, I was still faced with the calculus problem I couldn't figure out, and I still had too much homework and not enough hours to finish it. My life was just as out of control as it was before I ate, except, afterward, in addition to feeling frustrated, I also had guilt and remorse from having eaten food I didn't need.

To break free from the habit of eating in response to frustration, the key is to "let go and let God." Submit to him rather than trying to control everything yourself. You have nothing to lose when you do that. No matter what you'd like to believe, you're not lord over the people and situations that frustrate you, anyway. *Jesus* is Lord. And he's better at controlling things than you are—no offense.

When you accept that it's okay not to have control, you don't mind it as much when you feel out of control. And that decreases the strength and frequency of the emotions that trigger you to eat to regain control. Voila! True submission to God is slimming!

Anxiety

To escape from anxiety, which is a form of fear, some people *eat*. I should know, because I used to be one of those people.

I already mentioned that, at Cornell, I used to stress-eat, especially during exam week because of the extra academic pressure. However, I didn't mention yet that dating caused me anxiety too. It occasionally led me to eat as a defense mechanism when I wasn't actually hungry.

All it took was a few frat parties and a few trips to the college-town bars for me to realize that I had conflicted feelings about thinness. On the one hand, I felt good about being more attractive. But on the other hand, I felt scared of the consequences. If a drunken college boy looked at me with piggish lust in his eyes, or if he said something lewd, it made me feel vulnerable. A few times it almost made me wish I were fat again.

Losing weight made me feel like I had lost a layer of protection. Since men are physically larger and stronger than I, how would I protect myself walking home from the library late at night? How could I keep men away if I didn't want their attention? What if my physical boundaries weren't respected on a date? How would I defend myself, being so small? Maybe it would be safer to be unattractive.

Occasionally my feelings of vulnerability led me to binge after a night on the town, I guess in an unconscious attempt to fatten myself back up to a point where I felt safe.

Even though on the surface I thought I wanted to be thin, my unconscious fear of being attractive was sabotaging my weight-loss success. It was yet another unconscious tug-of-war, like the one Paul talked about, and it made it harder to control my weight.

First, regarding my anxiety about being physically threatened, God provided me with resources so I could learn to use *words* to convey the message I previously relied on my fat to convey. I learned to say things like, "Would you mind not standing so close to me," or "I don't really like it when you put your arm around me like that," or "I feel uncomfortable when you say things like that." Consequently, I felt empowered and experienced fewer impulses to eat to surround myself with a layer of protection.

Second, God allowed me to realize that I was not responsible for the thoughts that drunken young men had about me at frat parties or in bars. Their thoughts were their problem. All I had to worry about were my thoughts and my choices, so I made the choice to stop going to those places.

Third, God allowed me to let my guard down and feel fear and anxiety more directly, without having to eat to avoid those emotions. When I began to experience my emotions more directly, I discovered that fear and anxiety were not actually lethal. Since I survived after experiencing those emotions, I no longer feared experiencing them. That, in turn, decreased my urge to eat to avoid them.

Fourth and finally, God revealed the most important information of all: no matter how my emotions lied to me, and no matter how physically vulnerable or sturdy I imagined myself to be, *he* was, is, and always will be in control.

Anger

One day Bob made a mistake at work and was yelled at by his boss, who happened to be a woman. Even though Bob temporarily suppressed his anger, he did not process it and let it go like Paul instructed in Ephesians ("'In your anger do not sin': Do not let the sun go down while you are still angry, and do not give the devil a foothold" [4:26–27]). Instead, Bob quietly stewed on his anger until, on his break an hour later, he stuffed it down further with a couple candy bars, a bag of chips, and a can of pop.

Let's try to figure out what Bob did wrong so we can learn from his example.

First, Bob believed that he was sinning if he felt angry, even if he didn't yell at or hurt anyone in response to it. Therefore, he dealt with his anger in the only way he knew. He ate it. He literally stuffed his anger inward with food.

However, Bob was wrong. It is not a sin to feel angry. It's even okay, in some cases, to act outwardly on it. Jesus, who was sinless, angrily overturned the money changers' tables at the temple (Matthew 21:12–13). David killed Goliath for mocking God in 1 Samuel 17:45–47. And God himself killed people in anger.

Do you see the difference between the biblical examples and Bob's example, though? Bob's anger was self-centered, whereas the biblical examples are God-centered. Bob's pride was hurt when his boss yelled at him, and that led him to eat to regain a sense of control.

To make matters worse, Bob was yelled at by a female superior, and that caused him to feel even more emasculated and weak than if a male superior had yelled at him.

Like many men, Bob confused "My pride is hurt" with "I'm angry." Thus, in response to feeling weak and injured, he reached for something he could control so he could feel more powerful, and that something was food.

As is often the case, Bob's anger was influenced by experiences from his past. As a child, he was verbally abused by his mother, and when his boss (a female in authority) yelled at him, he literally went back into little-boy mode and repressed (or ate) his anger to avoid further abuse.

Now let's look at what Bob could have done differently.

Bob stewed on his emotions when he should have prayed for guidance. In prayer, he could have asked, "Lord, help me identify the emotion that I feel right now. Is it anger? Where does my deepest anger come from? Somewhere in my childhood? Could this current situation with my boss have triggered a hurt part of me from the past? Did she hurt my pride? Does she remind me of somebody? Am I angry because I feel out of control? Weak? Powerless? Stupid? Like I did when I was a kid?"

Once you explore the roots of your anger and understand your triggers from the past, you'll be better equipped to deal with anger you feel in the future.

Furthermore, Bob could have asked, "Why can't I just sit here and feel angry, anyway? Why do I need to distract myself from my emotions by eating? Lord, please help me to sit here and fully experience anger without eating in response to it."

Another thing Bob could have done is release his anger through physical activity at the end of his work day. He could have taken it out on the treadmill. Or he could have gone for a brisk walk. Exercise not only reduces stress, but it also boosts the level of certain brain chemicals that can help calm your negative emotions.

Finally, Bob could have prayed for his boss. You can't stay mad at somebody you pray for. Eventually you see them through the eyes of God's love and mercy.

If you want to lose weight and keep it off, pay attention to your emotions. Name them. If the emotion is anger, discern whether it is justified, God-centered anger or if it is self-centered. In other words, identify the *root* of your anger. Simply connecting the dots and identifying the root of your anger can help you to let go of it more easily.

The Common Denominator: The Desire for Control

Did you notice that the four emotions I have mentioned (stress, frustration, anxiety, and anger) all have something in common? They are all linked by your desire to feel in control.

That's the exact same impulse that got Lucifer kicked out of heaven, and it's the same desire that led Adam and Eve to eat the forbidden fruit. They wanted the same power and control God has.

How do you combat this desire to be in control? You have to keep reminding yourself of the truth: no matter how capable and in charge or how terribly out of control you *feel*, it's all just a façade. You aren't in control, anyway. *God* always was and always will be the one who is in control. He has absolute power, knowledge, and control over you and over the people and situations that frustrate you.

It's easy to fall into the illusion you're in control because it feels good. It puffs up your ego. The lie is more appealing than the truth. But you must choose the truth anyway because the lie will destroy you.

In my case, when I found the antidote (remembering God is in control and I am not), he gave me immediate relief from the negative emotions that led me to overeat. It was like a tremendous burden was lifted off me. All of the pressure I put on myself went right out the window.

He revealed another liberating truth to me, as well: it's not a bad thing to have empty God-shaped spaces left over from childhood. If he allowed us to grow up with no hurts or deficiencies, then we might never become desperate enough to seek him for completion and salvation.

I'm saying that *because* of our imperfect childhoods, we are left with incentives to seek him. If that's the case, then we ought to thank God for our empty spaces, unmet needs, hurts, and traumas, just as Paul thanked God for the thorn in his flesh in 2 Corinthians 12:7. Perhaps without our brokenness, we wouldn't have asked Jesus to save us!

For some reason, once I started thanking God for giving me areas of weakness, especially in regard to food, my weaknesses didn't bother me as much anymore. It didn't even bother me so much that I was imperfect. It is for my own good that I am imperfect and not in control, because, as it says in 1 Corinthians 12:9, his power is made perfect in my weakness.

Depression

I've worked in the medical specialty of pain management for ten years. In my line of work, I've found that most of my patients are depressed.

Because of my interaction with so many people who suffer with depression, I've come to appreciate how incredibly complex it can be to treat. Depression is also hard to write about for that same reason. You can't analyze it in a couple pages in a book and expect to solve the problem just like that.

So please be generous with me as I only touch upon this subject. I realize that my insights won't necessarily cure your depression. But if I uncover some little pearl of wisdom that alleviates your burden a little bit, then I'll consider it to be a success. Every little bit helps, right?

First of all, what is depression? Most people view it as being in a state of deep and unrelenting sadness beyond the normal ups and downs in life. Many believe that it is due to a chemical imbalance in the brain involving the neurotransmitter serotonin. And most doctors (like me) believe it should be medicated when it significantly interferes with a person's functioning.

Depression causes you to feel worthless and guilty. You lose interest in the activities you once enjoyed, you suffer disturbances in your sleep, you either withdraw or become agitated, you have trouble concentrating, you develop bodywide aches and pains, and you either gain or lose weight.

If food is not your crutch, you will probably withdraw from eating, just as you withdraw from other pleasurable activities due to the depression. Then you will lose weight. If food *is* your crutch, well, you know what happens. You try to narcotize your negative emotions with food, and you gain weight.

When it comes to depression, once again, the issue of feeling out of control is relevant. Depression can be reinforced by the feeling that a person has no control over his or her life, at least according to the definition of depression as being a form of learned helplessness. Because deep down you feel worthless, guilty, and ashamed of your lack of control, you reach out to something else that you want to control, like food.

As previously mentioned, dieting in the traditional way might make your depression worse. When you diet, you become even more aware of the fact that you have no control at all. According to research, you have an 80 percent chance of failing,[1] which suggests that you also have an 80 percent chance of compounding your depression with additional feelings of helplessness.

Are you ready for some good news now? It's called antidepressant medicine. If your doctor suggests that you take it for your depression, go ahead and do it. So what if you think it's cheating? As DuPont used to say, "Better living through chemistry." Once you have the right chemical balance in your brain, it will make it easier for you to dwell on, receive, and then act on the truth of God as it is revealed to you through this book.

Guilt

When I was an obese kid, I received this message loud and clear from the world around me: "You're fat and inadequate. You should constantly try to lose weight so you can be normal."

Even after I lost weight, this message stuck with me like white on rice. No matter what I weighed, I believed I wasn't thin enough. I believed I had to continue the diet indefinitely.

Thus, I felt guilty if I ate fattening food—even when I was hungry.

How did I get around my guilt? I used rationalizations. If I ate cookies, I only ate the broken pieces, because they seemed to not count as "real" cookies. Never mind that I ate twenty pieces, equaling eight whole cookies.

Likewise, if I ate the cake sitting on the kitchen counter, I only cut slivers off of it: one sliver each of the fifteen times I passed the cake. By the end of the day, I had eaten two whole pieces in the form of slivers. Duh! It's no wonder I gained weight when I was eating to avoid guilt. I was eating in a piecemeal way, not really enjoying or acknowledging the food. Unfortunately, this meant I wasn't satisfied by it, either.

Ironically, guilt not only can make you fat, but it can also keep you fat. It can keep you from approaching God for help with weight loss.

Face it: it can feel downright petty to ask God for weight loss when other people are dying of starvation, living with cancer, and facing all kinds of other hardships.

But God knows your embarrassing weaknesses whether you admit them or not. And, because he is all powerful, he perceives all of your requests the same way: they are all easy. I guess that's why Paul said in Philippians 4:6 that you should ask God for anything—even something as seemingly trivial as weight loss.

Besides, if you've already confessed your sins and repented, you don't even have a reason to feel guilty anymore. Your sin is gone. It's at the bottom of the ocean (Micah 7:18–19). In God's mind, it doesn't even exist anymore.

Shame

Some people confuse guilt and shame. Guilt is feeling bad about something that you did or did not do, whereas shame is feeling bad about who you are. For example, you may feel guilty about eating too much cake, but you feel ashamed of being a bad person because you ate the cake. Guilt is about the *doing* and shame is about the *being*.

Consider the shame some of us feel because of our inability to control what we eat. If we didn't feel shame, we wouldn't go to such great lengths to hide our peculiar eating habits from our families and friends.

I recall a story told to me by a patient who cleans bathrooms for a living. She said that a couple times a week, she finds candy wrappers in the feminine products receptacles in bathroom stalls. It's usually multiples of the same kind of candy wrapper in each receptacle, suggesting that one person ate all the candy bars. However, she finds these wrappers at different facilities, suggesting that this is a common behavior.

Can you imagine the guilt and shame these poor women suffer?

Maybe you think this behavior is weird, but if you eat even one candy bar in your car as you drive and then get rid of the wrapper evidence, you do the same thing as those other women, only to a lesser degree.

If you want to be freed from the shame of overeating, then your solution is to not rely on your emotions, which mislead you into feeling ashamed, but to remember the truth: shame never comes from God. It comes only from the Accuser.

I'll tell you how to win at this game: show the Accuser who is boss. Say, "*Jesus* is Lord." Then rub Satan's face in the dirt still further: wait until you're hungry and eat that candy out in the open where people can see you. Eat it with a sense of entitlement, too, because Jesus said that all food is allowable to you. Moreover, eat only half of the candy bar, pay attention to it while you eat, and eat it to the glory of God.

Could Depression, Guilt, and Shame Be Rooted in Misperceptions?

Have you ever wondered if your perceptions and recollections from early childhood might be a little "off"? It would only make sense. You processed and stored those memories as a child, at a time when your reasoning skills were limited.

Since your childhood memories can reinforce the depression, guilt, and shame that lead you to overeat in your adult life, you should look at them with a more discerning eye. Check to see if your memories are laced with misperceptions or lies that Satan is using against you. Then you can get to the root of why you eat for the wrong reasons, and you can stand a better chance of succeeding at permanent weight loss.

Let's look at how childhood memories played out in the life of a woman I will call "Alice" in regard to her weight problem.

Throughout her life, Alice struggled with depression, guilt, shame, and habitual overeating. On the advice of her professional counselor, Alice prayerfully explored the root of the emotions contributing to her inappropriate eating behavior.

Before long Alice remembered her depression started after her younger sister died of leukemia. She recalled feeling guilty about not being able to donate bone marrow to save her sister's life. She even felt responsible for her sibling's death. As it turned out, Alice's overeating was a way to punish herself for not being able to save her sister's life.

Looking back on that memory objectively, and using adult reasoning skills, it's easy to find the distortion of the truth. In reality Alice was in no way responsible for her sister's death. It wasn't her fault that she wasn't a bone marrow match. The leukemia was just a bad thing that happened. Alice certainly did not deserve the punishment she was inflicting on herself.

On an intellectual level, as an adult, Alice was able to recognize that it was illogical to continue to blame herself for her sister's death. However, to some degree she continued to feel guilty anyway, and she continued to punish herself with overeating. Why would that be?

Alice remembered past events not only through her intellect but also through her emotions—in this case including the guilt and shame she felt as a child. Even though she knew on an intellectual level she didn't cause her sister to die, on an emotional level, she still felt guilty, because her childhood emotions were never "replaced" with the right emotions.

Consequently, Alice needed a new emotional experience to correct the old, distorted one and reframe it in truth. Put another way, Older Alice needed to look Young Alice in the eye, love her, hold her, reassure her, tell her the truth, and help her feel the truth—that her sister's death was in no way related to anything Alice did or did not do; it was just an inevitable part of life.

That's exactly what Alice did through professional counseling. By the grace of God, she made an emotional connection with her inner child and was able to *feel* vindicated from the guilt. As a result, she experienced diminished guilt in her adult life and had less frequent and less intense impulses to punish herself by gorging on food.

Like Alice, you may have depressive thoughts based on distortions of the truth, and maybe you continue to respond to them through your uncorrected childhood perceptions and emotions.

Maybe when you were a child, somebody told you negative things about you that weren't true, and maybe you still condemn and punish yourself for those things. If that's the case, you need to forget those messages because they're lies. Read the truth in Scripture, and then seek professional counseling so you can go back to your inner child and help her (or him) *feel* the truth in the situation.

You can then experience fewer emotional triggers that lead you to eat for the wrong reasons, and you can have an easier time losing weight and keeping it off permanently.

Boredom

You know how little children can be. They whine, "I'm bored," if they have to spend ten whole minutes *not* doing something interesting.

When I'm bored, I'm the same way, except I don't usually whine. I'm tempted to eat to break up the monotony. Eating something delicious causes my taste buds to become excited, and it offers me a momentary diversion from boredom.

Ironically, since overeating makes you fat, if you eat when you're bored, you inadvertently create another reason to not be bored: you have to occupy your time making amends for overeating. Either you have to spend extra time exercising, or you have to spend extra time searching for the right diet plan or the right diet recipe to erase your mistake. In a way, you become wrapped up in a cycle of first creating a weight problem, then having to solve it. Voila! The perfect distraction from boredom: a pathetic exercise in futility—creating problems and then trying to solve them.

I know I'm not alone on that one. I have high-strung, usually female patients who admit the same thing. We unconsciously create problems (even weight problems) just so we can focus our mental energy on solving them. Are we complex creatures or what?

The real question is why do we do that. Are we trying to keep busy to avoid thinking about something painful? Are we running from something? Do we have too much time on our hands? Why do we feel we have to have a problem or a goal to work on all the time? Why can't we just sit still and be? I believe we're often afraid of confronting our emotions head-on, and this has to change if we expect to lose weight and keep it off.

Loneliness

Maybe you have an empty nest—or just the opposite, you are isolated due to the birth of a baby. Illness, divorce, job loss, retirement, the death of a loved one, or a move to a different city all can cause feelings of loneliness. But if your loneliness leads you to reach for food as a replacement friend, then I'll just tell you right now: it doesn't work. Food can't replace lost human relationships.

If you want to feel less lonely, then lean on God, allow yourself time to grieve your loss, and then reach out to other people for support. The reason you need other people is that neither God nor food can give you warm, human hugs, and neither can look you in the eye and say, "I love you." You can only get those things from real, live people.

For starters, look for close relationships in your own church. If you belong to a larger church, you might have the opportunity to join a smaller, home-based group. It's easier to deepen relationships in a more intimate setting like that. Some churches even have special-care groups, such as those for young mothers or seniors, for those going through divorce, or those recovering from various other obstacles in life, like addiction or abuse.

On the other hand, perhaps you're lonely in spite of the fact that you're *already* busy and surrounded by people who love you. This would suggest that your problem lies in your thinking and in your perceptions. In that case, ask, "Lord, I'm surrounded by people who love me, yet I feel lonely. Could there be something else I'm missing?" Ask him to reveal where your perceptions and emotions may not line up with the truth.

It is also possible that you're lonely because you aren't satisfied by your current relationships. If so, pray for understanding as to why you feel that way. Maybe the answer is you feel incomplete and you lay perfectionist, impossible-to-satisfy expectations on others when you should lean on God to complete you.

On the other hand, maybe the other people in your relationships really have fallen short, and you need to pray for them to be reconciled with God. Pray for yourself, too. Ask God to help you *perceive* the ones who let you down in a more favorable way, with mercy and love rather than disappointment. It will be good for *you* to do that.

Fatigue

Another emotion that can lead you to eat for the wrong reasons is fatigue. When you have a really demanding day, you might rationalize, "Well, I deserve this piece of pie. I just worked really hard to take care of everyone else, and now I want to do something for myself." However, Jesus did not say, "Come to me, all you who are weary and burdened, and I will give you *pie*." He said he would give you rest (Matthew 11:28).

If you eat because you feel physically or intellectually tired, you probably already know that eating doesn't replenish you in the long run. You just end up feeling equally exhausted, but in a bigger body.

Your better solution is to ask God, "What is really draining me of energy?" If you are physically tired, perhaps you need physical rest. If you are emotionally tired, ask God to provide you with emotional restoration. If you are intellectually tired, maybe you need a restorative, mindless diversion like watching a movie or going for a walk.

All the food in the world won't make you feel better if the thing you need is something other than food. Figure out what you really need by asking God, and then try to meet that need directly.

"What You're Missing Is Not in Here"

To avoid eating because you're bored, lonely, or fatigued, write this on a piece of paper and put it on your refrigerator: "What you're missing is not in here!"

Do you remember how Satan tempted Adam and Eve? He got them to compare themselves to God. He led them to believe that they were missing something (the power God has). In so doing, Satan created an empty space in them that didn't previously exist. Then Satan convinced them that eating the forbidden fruit would fill the empty space that he created.

Interestingly, Satan still uses the same tactics on us. He either creates or capitalizes on the feeling that we are missing something by getting us to compare ourselves to somebody else. We think, "Gosh, I wish I were slim like her," when the truth is the other person just has different problems. She may even be worse off than we are, overall, but we don't know because we only see her pretty, well-groomed exterior.

When we feel tired, lonely, or bored, Satan leads us to believe that the thing we are missing is food. Then he tells us that eating will make us feel better.

I recently experienced this kind of temptation at work. I had a particularly hard day, and I was worn out by midafternoon. Not wanting to deal with the emotionally draining patient who was waiting on me, I wandered into the break room to escape. I didn't realize it, but I was looking for something I was missing—a reprieve, maybe.

I didn't find a reprieve in the break room. I found doughnuts. When I saw them, I momentarily thought, "Aha! Doughnuts! That must be what I didn't know I needed! They sure look delicious. Should I or shouldn't I?"

Thankfully, I didn't take the bait. I caught myself just in time. I thought, "Wait a minute; I'm not even hungry. I just wanted to avoid Mrs. So-and-so for a while. And what was I thinking when I came in here when I wasn't hungry, anyway? Duh! Next time I'm looking for a diversion, I'll avoid the kitchen altogether."

So put that note on your refrigerator or on the table next to the doughnuts. "What you're looking for is not in here!" When you wander to the fridge or to the box of doughnuts because you feel you're missing something, turn around and go to your Bible instead. That's where you'll find real emotional restoration.

Eating in Response to Positive Emotions

Sometimes, if we feel particularly good, we like to augment our good feelings with food. If we accomplish something special, we can't count on anybody else to give us the "Atta girl!" or "Atta boy!" that we deserve, so we take charge and buy a candy bar. If we're at a party and everybody else is eating and drinking and laughing, we feel more *connected* with them if we're eating too.

That's especially true if we consume alcohol during the festivities. Alcohol stimulates the appetite and lowers inhibitions that restrain us from overeating.

Take my advice: if you want to reward yourself for an accomplishment or if you want to celebrate with others, think of non-food-related ways to do it. Buy a new outfit, spring for a one-hour massage, or splurge on a gym membership. If you're at a celebration that involves food, stay away from the buffet table if you're not hungry. Find somebody to talk to who is not eating.

Learning those habits will help you to dissociate food and rewards.

In the long run, you need to think of food as being for hunger, rather than being for anything else.

Weight Gain Following
Emotional Shock or Trauma

Being that I'm a pain management physician, I've treated patients with emotional as well as physical injuries that result from motor vehicle collisions, work-related injuries, orthopedic trauma, widespread burn injuries, amputations, debilitating or terminal illness, and physical and/or sexual abuse. I've treated Oklahoma City bombing victims (and their family members), and I've treated soldiers, police officers, and fire fighters who were injured in the line of duty.

Through these patient encounters, I've observed that when trauma-related emotional scars remain buried in our unconscious minds, Satan uses them as weapons against us. He does so through his characteristic lies, "You're never going to get well—you're going to hurt forever," "You're not a real man [or woman] if you can't work anymore." "You're worthless. All you do is lie around and take pain medicine."

Sometimes, Satan's lies are geared to cause anxiety or fear. "You almost died in that car wreck. Now, you'll never feel safe again in a car." Or, "You were almost killed in a surprise attack during the war [or at a freak accident at your job]. Some other random, unexpected threat could strike you [or those you love] at any time."

I bring these issues up in a weight-loss book for a very important reason. If Satan's lies and your hidden trauma-induced emotional hurts motivate your overeating, you need to identify and be purged of those problems in order to lose weight and keep it off permanently.

In my ten years of practice, I've met numerous patients who gained substantial amounts of weight after sustaining physical and/or emotional trauma. In most cases, my patients didn't realize the full contribution of the trauma to their weight problems until I pointed it out to them.

In the short term, eating distracted them from the underlying pain, fear, and anxiety after their trauma. However, in the long term, eating caused weight gain and even more anxiety. The idea that "food will make you feel better" was just another one of Satan's lies.

How about you? Did you begin to gain weight within weeks to months after you suffered emotional or physical trauma? If so, think about how that affects your prognosis for long-term weight loss. If you eat to distract yourself from your buried pain, how will you deal with those issues after you lose weight? What will be your new crutch? How will you address that pain?

In order to achieve and maintain long-term weight loss, a person has to deal not only with the surface condition, or the symptom of the disease (the overeating), but also the underlying cause. In other words, you have to be healed deep down, so that you no longer need a crutch.

How do you identify if a deep-down hurt leads you to overeat? Ask yourself, "What happened in the few months before I started gaining weight?" In many cases, the answer will be obvious, "I was in a traumatic car wreck and had a long, horrific hospitalization," "I was served with divorce papers," "My husband was deployed to the Middle East," or "I lost my job and began to feel worthless." Sometimes simply identifying the underlying emotional trigger can decrease its ability to lead you to overeat.

In other cases, you may not be able to think of an immediate trauma that triggered or aggravated your eating problem. Even so, God knows the answer, so ask him through prayer. Perhaps he will direct you to a medical professional or Christian counselor for treatment.

Other Methods to Combat Emotional Eating

A variety of therapeutic approaches exist for dealing with emotional issues from a Christian point of view. I wish I could tell you about all of them, but, honestly, I don't know about all of them. Thus, I'll tell you about the techniques that I've observed to work quickly and dramatically for my patients, and I'll leave you to research the other techniques on your own.

The most effective methods I've seen for achieving permanent release from emotional bondage include Theophostic Prayer and other subtypes of Christian Inner Healing Ministries. These techniques seek to replace the Accuser's lies that are buried in a person's unconscious thinking with the light of God's truth.

For example, I've had patients who have believed, on some deep, unconscious level, that they must be perfect to be acceptable to others, or that the death of a parent or the abuse suffered by a parent was their fault, or that they are bad or dirty or shameful due to a history of sexual abuse. Christian inner healing helped them find their "hurt inner-child selves" so that, through unified prayer with the counselors, they could receive revelation of God's truth.

What kind of truth am I talking about? Generally, the truth is opposite to the lies they previously believed. In the case of the aforementioned patients, God revealed to them in the midst of the counseling sessions that they don't have to be perfect, that the death of the parent wasn't their fault, and that they are not dirty or shameful.

Though I have never once seen a patient harmed by these techniques (in fact, my personal observation is a 95 percent success rate), some Christians consider these counseling techniques to be controversial.

I believe the main argument against these inner healing practices is that some less experienced practitioners might inadvertently make "suggestions" about the client's past when the patient is in a vulnerable state. For example, the inexperienced counselor might lead a client to "remember" that he or she had been sexually abused as a child, when, in reality, no actual abuse occurred.

However, keep in mind that that phenomenon is possible in any form of counseling. Any inexperienced practitioner, Christian or otherwise, could potentially make false suggestions such as these. So exercise care in choosing a counselor that has a good reputation.

I've also had patients see Christian counselors who incorporate secular, but nonetheless highly effective, techniques such as EMDR and Emotional Release Techniques. These techniques help to identify lie-based thinking, and many are likely to be helpful when delivered by a caring counselor (Christian or otherwise) who is attuned to you. Remember: God can use non-believers to help you too.

For more information on these healing ministries, check out www. Theophostic.com or search the internet for "Christian Inner Healing," "EMDR," or "Emotional Release Techniques."

Conclusion

If you are tempted to eat in response to your emotions, recall that eating in response to stress, anger, frustration, and anxiety is rooted in the desire to feel you are in control. You can fight the urge to eat unnecessarily by remembering your rightful place in the hierarchy: *subordinate* to God. He is in control and you are not. So relax and let him do his job.

If you are tempted to eat in response to guilt, shame, or depression, then your answer is to stop dwelling on your perceived past mistakes. Your memories may be laced with lies that cause you to be unduly hard on yourself. You know that the Accuser is behind that tactic, so don't blindly trust the emotions that he is trying to manipulate you with. Dwell on the truth of God instead and know that you are worthy because you are a child of the King.

If you are tempted to eat by feelings of loneliness, fatigue, or boredom, remember that those emotions can mislead you into feeling you are missing something that somebody else has, when, in fact, the person you envy is no better off than you are. If you're missing something other than food, then all the food in the world won't make you feel better. Know that what you really need is companionship, rest, or some other diversion.

The key to taking control of these potentially misleading emotions is to differentiate your feelings from the absolute truth in the situation. You may feel like eating in response to emotions because you learned to handle your emotions that way, but the truth is your body may not need food at the time. If you feel like eating in response to emotion, remember what you know to be true: food satisfies only physical hunger. God satisfies emotional and other hungers.

In addition, ask God, through prayer, to help you experience negative emotions less frequently, to help you disassociate your emotions from the learned response of eating, and to help you find better resources for dealing with your negative emotions, like exercise or doing the audio relaxation exercises titled "Godly Affirmations for Weight Loss."

Finally, be open to the idea that your excess weight may not be your primary problem. It may be a symptom of a deeper problem that stems from underlying shock, trauma, anxiety, depression, or other emotional issues. If that is the case, then pray for God to either heal you directly through prayer, or to be a "lamp unto your feet" and lead you to a Christian counselor, perhaps one who is familiar with Christian Inner Healing.

Temptation-Fighting Tools

*The biggest seller is cookbooks
and the second is diet books —
how not to eat what you've just
learned how to cook.*

Andy Rooney

One of my favorite patients needed a painful injection one day. Because I'm such an incredibly nice doctor (humble, too), I tried to engage him in conversation about something—anything, to take his mind off the shot. I decided to tell him about my book. Why not? It had to be better than the pain, or so I thought.

As I gave him the injection, I talked about the temptation story. "Satan couldn't have manifested as any other animal. He had to be a snake," I said, "because snakes don't have arms and legs. They can't hold people down with their tiny little snake hands and force them to eat forbidden fruit. The only weapon talking snakes have is their voice. They can only make suggestions. And then their victims have to choose how they respond in the face of the assault."

I thought I was being profound. I also thought my patient would get a kick out of the image of a snake holding a person down using tiny little snake hands and force-feeding them forbidden fruit. But he didn't, really. Maybe it was because the injection hurt, or maybe it's because the image wasn't as funny as I thought it was.

Deep down, most of us know that the devil can't make us eat when we're not hungry, and he can't make us eat too-large portions. Since he has no hands, he can only suggest, and then we have to use our own hands to carry out the deed. The truth is we have choices. We can either give in to temptation, or we can choose to fight it.

In this chapter, I will share with you some of the tools I use to make the right choices when I'm tempted to eat unnecessarily by that little snake voice in my head. I'll talk about how to control your thoughts, how to deal with sinful impulses, how to filter out temptation in advertising, and how to beat temptation using self-discipline and healthy distractions.

"For as [a Person] Thinketh in His Heart, So Is He"
(PROVERBS 23:7 KJV)

You must control your thoughts if you want to control your weight. Otherwise, your thoughts may wander to the dark side and lead you into temptation.

It might seem hard—or impossible—to choose what you dwell on, but you probably already do it without realizing it. Otherwise, God wouldn't have said (through Paul), "Set your minds on things above, not on earthly things" (Colossians 3:2).

Here is an example of how you may control your thoughts when you have an incentive to do it: pretend you and your spouse are alone in your Sunday school classroom, waiting for the class to arrive. On this particular morning, you are furious with your spouse because of something that happened the night before. In fact, the two of you are arguing.

However, the minute your Sunday school teacher walks into the room, you feel compelled to pull yourself together and calm down. After all, it would be embarrassing if he saw you arguing—especially at church.

To calm down, you pleasantly make small talk. Eventually, your anger passes. But when you get into the car to go home, you may make a conscious effort to get angry with your spouse again so you can finish (or I should say, win) the argument.

My point is, if you can turn off your anger when your Sunday school teacher walks into the room and then turn it on again later, you can also control your thoughts—and that means you can control your thoughts about food.

When you gain control over your thoughts, you automatically gain control over your emotions. Your emotions influence your choices, and, indirectly, influence your eating habits. In turn, your eating habits influence the amount of food you take in, and, therefore, determine your body weight.

Do you see the connection? Ungodly thoughts about food are fattening. There may be nine calories in a gram of fat and four calories in a gram of sugar, but there can be five thousand calories in one hour's worth of misplaced thoughts. Trust me; I've been there.

Now I'm going to give you some practical tips for controlling your thoughts about food. First, commit yourself to paying attention to what goes through your mind. Monitor your thoughts. When you catch yourself thinking about food, ask if you're hungry or if the idea to eat originated somewhere outside your stomach.

Second, when those poisonous, destructive thoughts pop into your head, trap them, hold them captive, and rebuke them. But don't rebuke them with your own willpower. As I said before, your human willpower can be fragile. You must use Scripture to rebuke those thoughts.

My favorite Scripture for rebuking negative thoughts about food is "Jesus is Lord" (Romans 10:9), as you might have already guessed. Dwell on that and other Scripture verses as often as possible, every day. Think about Scripture when you are tempted to eat, and soon you will undergo a renewing of your mind with godly thinking, as is alluded to in Romans 12:1–2.

After you rebuke your improper thoughts about food, choose to think about something more important. Read Colossians 3. It tells you exactly what you're supposed to think about. It even talks about how you get into bondage when you think too much about earthly things.

Or read 1 Corinthians 13, which discusses the nature of love. Or read any other passage from the Bible. It's all good and wise and important information.

Realize that when you eliminate a negative thought from your mind, you must replace it with a positive thought. Don't leave a hole in your mind where that negative thought once was, or another negative thought might fill it.

Choose to think positively. Dwell on what is right and good and truthful (i.e., Scripture), and the negative thoughts will have a harder time penetrating your mind. You can only dwell on one thing at a time, right? If you're thinking about what is good and right, you can't also entertain harmful thoughts, like wanting to eat when your body doesn't need food.

It's also good to think positively because your thoughts determine your emotions. If you dwell on the negative, you feel negative, and if you dwell on the positive, you feel positive. If negative emotions tempt you to eat, then you can derail those feelings by dwelling on God's love, mercy, faithfulness, righteousness, and kindness. If you change your mind, you change your emotions, and you'll be less likely to eat for emotional reasons when you're not hungry.

Did you get that? I'm saying that you don't have to put so much effort into fighting temptation anymore. You just have to choose to think about food the way God intended, and then the temptation will deflect off you like water off a duck's back.

Choose to Not Weigh Yourself All the Time; It Can Be Discouraging

In the first week of a reducing diet, you generally lose quite a bit of weight. Not realizing that you lost mostly water, you might feel extraordinarily good about yourself, perhaps even puffed up with pride over what you think is a big fat loss.

As time passes, your puffed-up self starts wearing down from all the stress. At your weakest point, your restraint breaks down and you cave in and cheat or maybe even binge.

As a result, you have a twofold problem. First, dieting caused your metabolism to become much better at storing fat. Second, if you binged, you consumed more calories than you needed.

As you might expect, by the next day, you will have gained a large amount of weight. However, you didn't gain much fat. You mostly gained water.

Not realizing the truth about the relative amounts of fat versus water you gained, you think, "It took me two weeks to lose five pounds and I gained three in one day. I might as well give up. Where's that box of chocolates?"

What you don't realize is that the whole situation is a lie. Due to water weight fluctuations, you didn't lose as much fat as you thought early on in the diet, and you didn't gain as much fat as you thought later on the binge. Still, you ended up feeling completely demoralized, defeated, and depressed. It's exactly what the Enemy wanted.

What's the solution? Break free from bondage to the scale. Stop weighing yourself all the time, and begin to measure success by how you feel emotionally and spiritually and by how your clothes fit.

Beat Sin by Doing the Opposite

Okay. Let's pretend your invisible force field momentarily breaks down because your mind is off of God and is fixated on your worldly obligations. And let's say you're tempted to eat when you're not hungry. How are you supposed to handle it?

Here's a novel idea: make the choice to do the opposite of what you're feeling urged to do. *Act* the way you want to be, and you will eventually *become* the way you want to be.

If you acknowledge that *gluttony* motivates you to overeat, then intentionally leave food on your plate in Jesus' name. Donate $20 a month to feed hungry children, get rid of your stashes of food, and choose to be the last one in line at the church potluck buffet. As I said, do the opposite of what your sinful nature tempts you to do.

If *greed* motivates you to eat all the food on your plate, remember that God loves you more than the food you're wasting. It would be better to throw the unnecessary food in the trash than to deposit it as fat on your abdominal organs. Besides, think about how much you will save in insurance co-pays at the doctor's office, at the pharmacy, and on your diagnostic tests once you lose weight and are cured of some of your medical problems.

If your problem is *disobedience*, make it a point to obey very quickly when God gives you the idea to stop eating. Don't sit there and argue with him in your mind about whether or not it's okay for you to take two or three more bites. Also, obey the four rules God gave you in the Bible regarding how to eat: don't worry about what you eat; you can eat any food; eat to his glory; and eat small portions so you're not gluttonous.

If your problem is *covetousness*, then stop restricting yourself from eating the foods you really desire. Eat what you enjoy in small portions when you're hungry, and then eventually you'll stop coveting fattening foods. Throw away your stashes of food. You know you can get more whenever you want. You don't need a storehouse anymore.

Purge your mind of worldly nutrition dogma and focus only on the four rules God gave you about how to eat. Listen for hunger pangs, and when you feel them, eat small quantities of the foods you enjoy.

If you offered yourself into *idolatry* to food and you bowed down to it, then "un-offer" yourself and stand up to it. Just take the time you used to engage in food-related thoughts and activities, and use it to think about and serve *him*. Tell the food, "Jesus is Lord and you are not." In addition, show the food who is boss by leaving some on your plate. Do the opposite of what you're tempted to do.

If your problem is *pride*, then stop comparing yourself to other people. As long as you are thinking about how round your face is, how many chins you have, or how fat you look in a swimsuit, you are distracted from God. So don't look at yourself or other people critically. Look at them and look at yourself through the eyes of love.

Realize that Satan wants you to have body image issues exactly so you will continue to be distracted from thinking about God. Instead of wanting a slim, sexy body for self-centered or prideful reasons, try to be a good steward of the temple God loaned to you for *his* sake, and commit your weight loss to *him*.

I am not the first one to recommend acting in an opposite way to your urges to overcome maladaptive habits. Modern-day psychologists recognize the same principle and say it in a different way. They say that your actions affect your attitudes. If you act in a certain way, even if it doesn't feel natural for you, you eventually get used to it, and your attitudes change to match. If you act like you don't care about food, eventually you truly won't care about it (as much).

At first the new behavior (making yourself wait to eat until you feel hungry and eating small portions) may not feel natural to you. Don't worry about that. Eventually you will get used to acting that way, and it will become your "new normal." It will feel more natural and less forced or intentional. Fake it 'til you make it, as the saying goes.

The apostle Paul said, "Only let us live up to what we have already attained" (Philippians 3:16). In other words, through Christ your weight-loss victory is *already won*, but whether or not it comes to fruition depends on whether or not you grab hold of your cure and start acting accordingly. "In the same way, faith by itself, if it is not accompanied by action, is dead" (James 2:17). So accompany your faith with action, and start thinking and acting like a thin person.

This Scripture verse means that you shouldn't wait to feel cured before you start acting cured. You may not see the heavens open up or feel the earth tremble the moment your cure begins, but you should go along with it anyway. Act like a thin person, and you'll eventually become one.

Think About Exercise
the Way a Child Does

As children, we couldn't hold still. But now, as adults, we don't want to move. We only run when there is a fire or if someone announces there is free food. If our doctor suggests that we should exercise, our heart rate goes up, but it's from sheer panic.

When it comes to exercise, kids are smarter than adults. Instinctively, they want to run around and burn off their hyperactivity after they have been cooped up in the house all day. But how do we adults let go of our tension after a long work day? We engage in sedentary activities that center on food, and we stress-eat.

We must consider our social activities to be more like childhood playdates. Instead of focusing on what kind of food we'll eat, we should focus on what kind of physical activity we can engage in. Why not play tennis, go bowling, go to the gym together, or engage in some other kind of physical activity we enjoy? Why does our family time have to be only at the dinner table?

Regarding what type of exercise to engage in, it's important to pick something that's fun and try to alternate between stretching (flexibility), weight lifting (resistance), and at least twenty minutes of aerobic exercise, which increases the heart rate.

If the weather is nice, get off the couch and go for a walk or ride your bike around the neighborhood. If the weather is bad, stay inside and exercise using an exercise video or stationary bicycle. It doesn't matter exactly what you do, just have fun, *get moving*, and commit your exercise to God just as Paul said you were supposed to do. (Remember he said to do everything to the glory of God in 1 Corinthians 10:31.)

If you are looking for cheaper suggestions than joining a gym, try these: if you have a sedentary job, then go for a brisk twenty-minute walk before you eat lunch. If you are unable to do that because of bad weather, then bring a set of small weights to work and pump iron in your office. Alternatively, use that time to stretch your muscles and save your aerobics for either before or after work. Unless you have bad knees or some other medical condition that limits your activity, take the stairs instead of the elevator. Instead of driving to a close destination, walk or ride your bike.

Don't you think it's ironic that our labor-saving devices, like elevators and cars, make us fat? And then, in turn, we have to drive to a gym to pay money to exercise on man-made machines?

In general, if we were more like children, we would play more, eat only when hungry, and be closer to the kingdom of God. Jesus said, "I praise you, Father, Lord of heaven and earth, because you have hidden these things from the wise and learned, and revealed them to little children" (Matthew 11:25).

The Benefits of Exercise

Study after study shows that exercise facilitates weight loss. However, did you know that you have to continue exercising if you want to keep the weight off once you lose it? To examine this subject further, let's look again at the National Weight Control Registry, which I mentioned briefly in chapter 6.

The National Weight Control Registry was created by researchers Rena Wing and James Hill in 1994, in an effort to survey the health habits of those who prove successful at long-term weight loss. Information about respondents' eating habits, degree of dietary restraint, exercise habits, etc., was obtained by a survey from over 4,000 successful losers of weight. To be included in the database, respondents must have lost an average of 72 pounds and kept it off over 5 years.

According to the data in the registry, in order to keep the weight off, successful females expended an average of 2,545 calories per week in physical activity, and successful males expended an average of 3,293 calories per week. The activities most preferred by registrants were walking briskly for one hour per day (76 percent), weight lifting (20 percent), cycling (20 percent), and aerobics (18 percent).[1]

Another study cites similar statistics. According to a 2002

Consumer Reports survey of thirty-two thousand dieters, four thousand "super-losers" were identified.[2] These were people who maintained a significant weight loss for five years or more. Eighty percent of those polled rated exercising at least three times a week to be their number one weight-loss strategy.

Not only can exercise speed your weight loss and help you to maintain it, it can also lift your depression. A study by J. A. Blumenthal showed that exercise was as effective as antidepressant medicine in ameliorating major depressive disorder in elderly subjects.[3]

There are several theories regarding why exercise is so beneficial from a mental health point of view. First, it triggers a sense of accomplishment. Second, it distracts us from our daily stressors. Third, it gives us increased social interaction.

Exercise also helps us to feel good physically. It causes the release of certain mood-enhancing brain chemicals, including endorphin, which is a natural painkiller that promotes a sense of well-being. It also relieves muscular tension, partly through an increase in local blood flow and possibly through raising the temperature of the muscle.

Earlier I mentioned the experiments on rats that had clips put on their tails to stress them. The stressed rats ate a lot more than unstressed rats when they were given unlimited food to eat. For me, exercising is like taking the clip off my tail. It helps me unwind. If I feel frustrated or angry and I go for a thirty-minute bike ride, I feel a lot better afterward and am much less likely to stress-eat.

Regarding your target heart rate and other medically relevant issues, such as determining what exercises you shouldn't do, consult with your doctor. If you are ill or if you have musculoskeletal limitations or pains, you may need to see a physical therapist to help you identify the exercises that best suit your individual needs. Or see a physical medicine and rehabilitation doctor, aka "physiatrist" (that's another name for my specialty). We specialize in rehabilitating people with musculoskeletal limitations and injuries. To find a doctor in my specialty, go to www.aapmr.org and click on the link to find a physiatrist in your area.

Regarding the intensity level of the exercise, start low and go slow. Ease into the program. The number one reason people give up exercise is that they do too much too fast and then get hurt. Many of them come see me with inflamed knees after they've lost twenty pounds, then I have to give them a steroid shot that makes them gain back ten.

Avert Your Eyes!

Every day on your way to work, you pass a billboard that says you get a free twenty-four–ounce steak if you can eat it all in one sitting. You even get unlimited salad bar visits with that steak, in case six times the amount of meat you need is not enough food for you. You've seen that billboard before and you know where it is. Stop staring at it.

Next you see a billboard for a Mexican fast-food restaurant. It says that you should eat a meal between dinner and breakfast. To make it seem more normal, they've coined the phrase "fourth meal," as though it's actually a word. You know where that billboard is too. Don't stare at it.

On the highway, there is a delivery truck in front of you with pictures of snack cakes all over it. You notice that you're staring at the pictures a little too long. Change lanes. Pretend the pictures are pornographic. Don't look.

At the grocery store, the magazines at the checkout stand are just as bad. They show pictures of cakes, cupcakes, and cookies. Ironically, below those pictures, the captions say, "Lose ten pounds by Friday by not eating dessert."

What those magazine covers are really saying is, "If you make this cake for your family, maybe, just maybe, you'll finally be a good enough wife and mother. But just remember to not eat any of it. You're too fat and need to be on a diet."

So what should you do? Consider the magazines to be pornographic as well, and don't stare at them. Avert your eyes just as you would if they showed pictures of naked people.

I'm not done griping yet about cakes and advertising. No, there's more. Last weekend I was in the process of baking the cake for a friend's baby shower. As the batter was whirling around in the mixing bowl, I was zoning, and my eyes wandered to the caption on the back of the box, where it said, "Bake up some fun!"

At first, I didn't think it was strange, but then, I had a huge "Aha!" moment. I realized it was part of the brainwashing scheme. Everywhere we turn, we are broadcast messages that we should look to food for our fun—even on the product labels themselves.

Here is my advice: to beat this kind of advertising-related temptation, you have to first recognize the temptation for what it is: a money-grabbing scheme. Then you have to *avert your eyes* from it. If you have a choice, don't look.

If you're watching television and a cooking show or food commercial comes on, get up and leave the room or change the channel. At the fast-food restaurant, don't look at the pictures when you order, or you might get confused and order too much. When you go to the price-club warehouse, walk right past the person giving out free samples without making eye contact (unless they talk to you first, of course).

Don't even look at the free glazed doughnut you're offered by the clerk as you walk into the doughnut shop. You know where it is; you can see it out of the corner of your eye in the clerk's hand. Instead, look the clerk in the eye and say, "No, thank you." Then order the exact doughnut that you went there for in the first place.

Of course, if you went in there for the glazed doughnut, then quickly snatch it out of the clerk's hand and run out the door before you're tempted to actually *buy* another one. Okay, I'm just kidding. But I think it would serve them right for tempting you.

Remember that Eve responded in part to the sight of the forbidden fruit, thinking that it looked good for food and pleasing to the eye. You might respond the same way to a picture of a triple-beef bacon cheeseburger combo meal on the picture menu, when all your body needs is one small, plain hamburger. So avert your eyes from the pictures and order a smaller meal from memory.

Do you know how to most easily avert your eyes from tempting food that you have in your house? Don't leave it out in the open where you can see it. Store it in opaque containers or put it in the cabinet. You've heard the saying, "Out of sight, out of mind"? Dr. Wansink actually proved this is true in terms of the visual cues that trigger us to eat.

In a very sneaky experiement, Dr. Wansink gave secretaries chocolates in two different types of candy dishes. Half of the secretaries received candy in dishes with see-through glass covers, whereas the other half got candy in dishes with opaque (non-see-through) covers. Which group do you think ate more candy? You guessed it! The group that could see through the lids into the candy dishes dipped into the stash 7.7 times per day, whereas the group that could not see through the lids dipped in an average of only 4.6 times a day. This translated into the first group eating seventy-seven more calories of chocolate per day,[4] which after one year would theoretically cause a gain of eight pounds of unwanted fat.

In another experiment, Dr. Wansink tested (or should I say, tempted?) a second group of secretaries, again with chocolate. This time, he placed the candy dish in different areas of the office, either wihin arm's reach on their desktops, stashed away in the desk drawers, or six feet away on a filing cabinet. In all cases, the candy was visible through the clear glass lid of the candy dish. The result was that if the secretaries had to get up to walk six feet to the filing cabinet, they ate less than half the amount of chocloate than when it was within arm's reach on their desktops.[5]

What is the take-home message here? The best place to store your junk food treats is not on top of your desk or kitchen countertop, but at the convenience store. Leave the junk food there and make a special trip to buy it if you want it bad enough. If you leave it lying around the house where you're more likely to see it, you're more likely to eat it when you're not actually hungry.

Let's say, for example, you're hungry for a snack cake. Figure out which one you want, go to the convenience store, and buy one. I mean *one*. Don't buy extra, because you don't need that temptation in the house. Then, when you get home, show the food (and yourself) that *Jesus* is Lord and eat only half. Save the other half for your next meal.

I'm saying you have to make it a point to reject the messages food advertisers send you, you have to avert your eyes from the pictures of food, and you have to avoid keeping too much tempting food in your house. Conquer your enemy in part by avoiding your enemy. Keep food out of sight, and it will be out of mind.

Use Awareness, Discipline, Scripture, and Distraction

Let's say that, before you read this book, you were in the habit of eating a candy bar right after lunch every day. You ate the candy both because it was a habit and because it tasted good, rather than because you were physically hungry for it.

Now you have increased awareness of your reasons for eating. Exactly because you *expect* and *recognize* the temptation, you are better equipped to resist it.

The temptation hits you right on schedule after lunch. Only now you know the truth: that it is Satan who is really talking when you think, "Go ahead. Eat the candy bar. You deserve it. You worked hard all morning. It's going to taste so good!"

Instead of reflexively caving in to the temptation, you react differently now that you are more aware. You turn away from the temptation and turn your attention to God, quoting Scripture like, "Get behind me, Satan! You are a stumbling block to me; you do not have in mind the concerns of God, but merely human concerns" (Matthew 16:23).

You might also say, "No weapon forged against [me] will prevail, and [I] will refute every tongue that accuses [me]" (Isaiah 54:17). I also like, "Away from me, Satan!" (Matthew 4:10) and "*Jesus* is Lord" (Romans 10:9, emphasis added).

Uh ... if you talk to the candy bar, you might look around first to make sure nobody is watching, because, well, you know, they'll think you're nuts.

Remind yourself that you can eat the candy bar the next time you feel true hunger pangs. Then, as previously mentioned, change your mind and think about better things. If you've already prayed and have other tasks that need to be attended to, do them. Intentionally look for a distraction. Go finish some paperwork you've been putting off. Pretty soon you'll forget all about the candy.

In this example, notice that you didn't fight the battle on your own. Just as Adam and Eve should have run to God to tattle on the serpent intruder, you should run to God when you are tempted, and let him fight off the bully for you.

Conclusion

To beat temptation, you have to exercise discipline and choose the path that is right, not the easier path or the path that appeals to your desire for pleasure. You have to be a better guardian of your thoughts than Adam was of the garden. This means you have to stop and think, "Am I physically hungry?" when the advertisements and sinful urges tempt you to eat.

If you are not physically hungry, you have to resist the urge to eat by averting your eyes, by controlling your thoughts, and by using Scripture and distraction as temptation-fighting tools.

Press On

The greatest oak was once a little nut
who held its ground.

Author Unknown

One of my favorite children's books is *The Little Engine That Could*. You probably remember it. It's the simple and beautiful story of a little engine that pulled a heavy train uphill by force of sheer will-power, saying "I *think* I can, I *think* I can," and then finally, "I *know* I can, I *know* I can." The moral of the story is that you can succeed if you keep your eyes on the goal and if you put forth your best effort.

I love that the story inspires children to achieve their goals. But as an adult, I've learned the story isn't complete. It takes a lot more than a short-lived, full-throttle climb up a single hill to succeed in life. You have to persevere in the long term. You have to endure the climb over multiple hills or obstacles, and you also have to be able to bounce back and keep trying over and over again when you fail.

In terms of weight control, some of us are like the little engine in the story. We're preoccupied with getting to the top of only one hill: we want to lose weight. Beyond that immediate goal, we have no long-term plan as to how to finish our journey. But the truth is, in the case of weight control, losing weight is just the beginning. Keeping the weight off can be more challenging than losing it.

How do you make it through the rest of your life without regaining weight? Basically, you need to undergo a renewing of the mind, such as Paul describes in Romans 12:1–2. You have to choose to replace your old ideas about food with scriptural truth, and you have to choose to eat small portions of food and only when you're hungry. The more you submit to God and choose to think about and do the right things, the easier it becomes to be transformed by him with renewed healthy attitudes about food and eating.

In this chapter I encourage you through your renewing of the mind to the point where you more consistently eat according to God's original plan: hunger pangs. That way you can stick to the Eden Diet for the long haul, lose weight, keep it off, and enjoy the abundant life that God promised to you.

First, I help you adopt the right attitude when you make mistakes and eat for reasons other than hunger. I help you to persevere in the face of adversity. Second, I offer advice that may help you discern the cause of the delay in your weight loss if you are sticking with the program but you are not seeing outward success. Finally, I encourage you to keep God in your focus and Scripture in your mind as you press on toward your goal.

Mental Transformation
Is a Lifelong Process

Why does it take so long to undergo a renewing of the mind about food? I suppose it's because we keep fighting against God.

In Romans 12:1–2, Paul told us to be like "living sacrifices" and submit to God to "be transformed." Well, the problem is, as living sacrifices, we tend to crawl off the altar. Every time we deviate from God and eat when we're not hungry, we take one or two steps in the wrong direction, toward the edge of the altar. We keep choosing to please ourselves sensually with food instead of choosing to please him, and that blocks our progress toward our goal.

It's okay, though. Believe it or not, it's biblical that a renewing of the mind can be a long, drawn-out process. In Romans 12:1–2, Paul says that if we submit to God we will "be transformed." But he uses the phrase in the present passive verb tense, which indicates that our transformation is designed to be an ongoing process rather than an instantaneous occurrence.

I like knowing that. In the twenty-five years since I lost weight, I've done my share of falling off the altar. However, Paul basically implied that it is okay; it's almost as if God expected it. Otherwise, he wouldn't have used the present passive voice. Isn't God merciful?

Paul talked about running a race to win (1 Corinthians 9:24) and he told us to "press on" (Philippians 3:14). Therefore, if we persevere and continue to seek God in spite of our mistakes, we will continue to be transformed until the day we die.

Choose Your Words Carefully

If you want to progress through a renewing of the mind about food, be careful about how you talk. Don't just guard what goes into your mouth; guard what comes out of it too.

Just as your actions affect your attitudes, what you say about yourself affects your beliefs. If you say, "I can't control myself around chocolate," then you basically plant the seeds of failure. You sabotage your own mental transformation. That's not just a Christian belief; it's basic psychology, too.

By speaking negative words aloud, you convince yourself that you're a failure. Don't do it. Instead, say things like, "I can eat chocolate any time I am hungry, but when I do, I enjoy it in small amounts as a luxurious gift from God."

Regarding your weight problem, plant the seeds of success. Say, "I used to eat for emotional reasons, but now I eat when I'm hungry." Don't say, "Hello, my name is Jane, and I am an emotional eater." Notice the difference between the two statements. The first one is past tense, and the second is present tense.

If you want to undergo a renewing of the mind, then cooperate with God as he transforms you. You have been made a new creation through Jesus Christ (2 Corinthians 5:17), so speak about your old self in past tense and your new self in present tense. Say things like, "At one time, I ate too much and I ate for the wrong reasons. Now I eat smaller portions of whatever I am in the mood for when I'm hungry, and I eat to the glory of God."

Remember that your actions affect your attitudes and your statements affect your attitudes too. So when you open your mouth, convince yourself of God's truth by speaking God's truth, whether or not it has actually come to pass yet.

Troubleshooting a Lack of Progress

If your weight loss has been slow, don't be discouraged. Think of the process as being like when a caterpillar metamorphoses into a butterfly. The earliest changes occur where only God can see, hidden away inside the cocoon. But eventually, a butterfly bursts forth and proves that important changes were happening on the inside, even if you couldn't see them from the outside.

I'm saying that God might have to change you on the inside, in your mind, before he can change you on the outside. Why? Maybe he knows something about you that you don't even know. Maybe you need the process to happen slowly for some reason. Maybe your metabolism needs extra time to adjust because you're medically frail, or maybe you have unresolved emotional issues that lead you to lean on your extra weight as a crutch. Maybe you have to work through those first. Only God knows the truth.

But if you haven't lost much weight yet, don't assume God wants you to stay heavy. It's quite possible you haven't fully stepped up to the challenge. Maybe you haven't cut back on your portion sizes enough. If you mastered the challenge of leaving one bite of each food on the plate, maybe you need to push yourself to leave five bites of food on your plate, and then ten, and then leave half of your food—or more.

In addition, maybe you need to wait awhile longer before you eat, experiencing your hunger pangs for longer and allowing your stomach to shrink. If you have been eating when you only feel the beginnings of hunger pangs, try waiting an extra half hour, and then an extra hour, and then two hours. During that time, distract yourself by becoming busy with other good tasks.

You might also need to exercise a little more intensely or for a longer period of time. If you have been walking for twenty minutes a day, then walk for thirty minutes, and ultimately sixty minutes altogether, and do it more briskly. Perhaps you should carry hand weights while you're at it.

If you're doing all of the above and you're still not losing weight, you might consider keeping a food diary and/or weighing and measuring your food, as I mentioned previously. There is a good chance you might be eating more than you think because you eat mindlessly or because you underestimate your portion sizes.

If you still aren't losing weight, perhaps you need more spiritual exercise, as well. Maybe you need to pray longer and harder and meditate more on God's Word. Perhaps the problem is you need to come face-to-face with your blessing-blocking sins, like idolatry, gluttony, greed, laziness, and the like, because they could be leading you to eat more than you need. Maybe if you confess and repent of those sins, your progress will be faster.

Remember: small victories add up. Every time you capture and divert a thought to eat for the wrong reasons, it results in your taking in fewer calories. Every time you leave food on your plate, you reinforce Jesus is Lord over you and food is not. Every additional minute you let your hunger pangs grow shows you have become even more disciplined. You can wait to eat because you are a mature adult. Every time you prefer healthy food over junk food, you show you are no longer in bondage to food.

Even if your weight loss does not materialize right away, know it will, and don't give up. Thank him anyway, according to these Scripture verses:

Though the fig tree does not bud
and there are no grapes on the vines,
though the olive crop fails
and the fields produce no food,
though there are no sheep in the pen
and no cattle in the stalls,
yet I will rejoice in the LORD,
I will be joyful in God my Savior.

HABAKKUK 3:17–18

Focus on the Road Ahead

It's not unusual for a person to experience a flood of revelation and success when they first start reading this book. Most of my patients lose six to ten pounds in the first month alone. That's when their weight-loss excitement is at its all-time peak.

But while many continue to achieve greater and greater success, for some the weight loss slows down and the excitement begins to wear off. About the time they reach a weight-loss plateau, some fall off course and regain some weight.

If that happens to you, don't fret and don't condemn yourself. And for goodness' sake, don't weigh yourself either. Just get back up on your feet, repent, keep praying, and keep asking him to reveal to you if you need to do something differently. If you stay the course, you will start to lose weight again.

You don't have to be perfect; you just have to be persistent. If you overeat at one meal, you have an opportunity to get back on track with the next meal. If you break down and overeat, you can interrupt the cycle at any time, by turning down your very next bite of food. There is no more "all or nothing." You don't have to start over the next day; you can start over immediately by putting the fork down at any moment.

Think about this example. When you are riding your bike, you focus your eyes on the road far ahead, rather than on the stretch of road right in front of you. If you veer a little to one side or the other, you make tiny adjustments with the handlebars so that you continue to approach the goal in the distance.

When you're riding your bike, you don't beat yourself up emotionally when you deviate a little bit here and there from the distant goal. You keep looking ahead with your eyes firmly fixed on your target, and eventually you get to where you want to be.

Be the same way when it comes to your weight-loss goal. If you deviate a little bit because you make mistakes and eat when you don't need to, don't sweat it. It's certainly not the end of the world. Just pick yourself up, dust yourself off, and start over again with the next bite of food you turn down when you're not hungry.

Why is it important not to dwell on your eating mistakes? First, it doesn't help in any way to dwell on the past. You can't change what happened in the past. You can only change the present and the future through the choices you make from now on.

Second, focusing on the past distracts you from God. Paul told you in Colossians 3 to dwell on heavenly things, and also to clothe yourself with mercy, compassion, forgiveness, and love. Therefore, apply those things to everybody who may have contributed to your weight problems, including yourself, and don't let Satan distract you with negativity. Just keep your eyes on the road ahead, dwell on Scripture, think positively, and keep pedaling.

Be Vigilant and Press On

As you forge ahead on the Eden Diet, be vigilant. No matter how healed you think you are, you must continue to guard your thoughts and your actions. Don't become complacent, thinking you are fully transformed and invincible. The minute you do, you're toast. Your flesh is still tainted with sin, and you are imperfect.

That's why Paul said we must be alert and quick to deal with the return of our sinful desires: "And we will be ready to punish every act of disobedience, once your obedience is complete" (2 Corinthians

10:6). And that's why Peter told us, "Be self-controlled and alert. Your enemy the devil prowls around like a roaring lion looking for someone to devour" (1 Peter 5:8 NIV). Or did he say, "The lion prowls around waiting for *you* to devour ..."?

You are a work in progress. As Paul said, "God, who has begun a good work within you, will keep right on helping you grow in his grace until his task is fairly finished" (Philippians 1:6, author's paraphrase). So "press on toward the goal to win the prize for which God has called [you] heavenward in Christ Jesus" (Philippians 3:14). Do that by eating small portions of food according to your hunger and by eating to the glory of God.

Conclusion

We shouldn't be surprised that restrictive dieting causes us to fail at weight control 80 percent of the time. It opposes God's natural plan for eating. It causes us to eat for external reasons rather than according to our hunger pangs. God gave us hunger pangs for a reason: to acknowledge them and respond to them in a natural way, by *eating*, rather than suppressing them and following worldly weight-loss dogma.

God told us exactly how to eat in the Bible. He told us not to be gluttonous (Proverbs 23:2); he told us not to worry about what we eat or drink (Matthew 6:25); he told us to eat to his glory (1 Corinthians 10:31); and he told us that all food was fit to be eaten (Mark 7:19). He even told us indirectly, through Paul, not to eat for the wrong reasons. He said, "Food for the stomach" (1 Corinthians 6:13). He didn't say that food is for medicating emotional or other nonphysiological needs.

If you lump all those divine instructions (and a few others) together into a weight-loss plan, it sounds like this: wait until you feel actual hunger pangs, eat small portions of any food you enjoy, and eat with joy and appreciation to his glory. Later, when you feel hunger pangs again, eat again, just as he designed you to do.

When you're not hungry, resist the temptation to eat by leaning on him through prayer. In addition, use Scripture as a weapon, avert your eyes from the temptation, control your thoughts, and find healthy distractions, like exercise.

In the beginning, God loved us so much that he set us free to make our own choices, such as whether or not we would obey him. We learned the hard way, starting with Adam and Eve's choices to eat the forbidden fruit and ending with our own sin, that disobedience brings nothing but failure. God's way is always the best way.

So, in the end, if we return to him and show him that we are truly his by submitting to him and by eating small portions of food and only when we're truly hungry, and if we fight temptation in the ways he advised, then we will surely be blessed beyond measure in the area of weight reduction.

Appendixes

Appendix A

Eating Disorders

Compulsive Eating

People who eat compulsively may experience intense, obsessive thoughts about food. Sometimes the thoughts are triggered by seeing or smelling or just thinking about the food. They may find it difficult to stop obsessing until they have some of whatever it is they are craving. After remaining fixated on this food for a period of time, such as days or weeks, they may then shift their obsession onto a different food.

Compulsive eaters may rationalize they don't have a problem as long as they are just thinking and not actually eating; however, the two go hand in hand. The obsessive thoughts result in compulsive overeating behaviors. Sometimes compulsive eaters have better control and diet effectively, but at other times they lose control and binge. As a result, their eating habits are erratic, they alternate between dieting and overeating or bingeing, and they gain weight in the process.

This erratic eating behavior is rooted in the need to control. In fact, the more compulsive eaters try to exert willpower to control their eating, the more they binge. They end up feeling food is lord over them, rather than the other way around.

To control their eating, they plan well in advance what they will allow themselves to eat. For example, they might start thinking about exactly what and how much they will have for dinner the moment they finish lunch. When they go to social events where there will be food, they plan in advance what and how they might eat because they are afraid of overeating. At the event, they spend more time and emotional energy dwelling on the food than enjoying the people.

When their restraint breaks down, they fall into periods of bingeing. During a binge, compulsive eaters may shovel enormous quantities of food into their mouths without truly tasting and enjoying it. They eat to the point of near explosion, and consequently they may feel physically ill.

Their bingeing occurs especially during nighttime hours and almost always when they are alone. Sometimes, during a binge, they have what are known as dissociative experiences, where they feel that they are not even mentally present while they are eating. They may suddenly realize they are standing at the refrigerator door eating a piece of pie, and they don't remember how they got there.

Perhaps they hide during a binge so nobody will see them, perhaps by eating in their cars or by eating hidden away in the bathroom stalls at work or school. They hide the wrappers, and they try to hide the guilt and remorse they stuff inside along with the food.

I want to point out the difference between having an obsessive-compulsive personality *type* and having an obsessive-compulsive personality *disorder*. First of all, every one of us has a personality type, and the obsessive-compulsive type is considered normal. In fact, most people who achieve worldly success tend to have it.

However, if your compulsive habits have a strong negative impact on your life, and if they severely affect your relationships or your job, you may have the *disorder*. If you suspect you have obsessive-compulsive personality disorder, you should seek medical attention and pray about taking certain medications that can lessen the symptoms.

While compulsive eating often leads to weight gain, you don't have to be heavy to have it. Some people remain thin when they have it, but that's because they binge less frequently or less severely, or perhaps they make up for their binges by overexercising. Still, the pathology in their thinking leads to tremendous suffering, whether or not you see the evidence of the disorder on the outside.

Anorexia and Bulimia

Anorexia nervosa is an eating disorder that, like compulsive eating, stems in part from the person's desire to control his or her environment. Anorexics feel powerless, and their response to these feelings is to find something to focus their control issues on. So, with distorted perceptions of being fat and excessive fear of gaining weight, they restrict themselves from eating and try to control their body shape to the point of emaciation.

By definition, anorexics are 15 percent or more below their ideal body weight and have missed three or more consecutive menstrual periods. They suffer from impaired social and psychological functioning and from physical consequences such as emaciation, brittle bones, anemia, heart and other organ failures, and even death.

Bulimia nervosa is an eating disorder that also stems from a desire to exert control. Bulimics are generally at normal weight, but may be slightly overweight. When triggered by unpleasant emotions, bulimics binge, subsequently feel guilt and shame, and ultimately use tactics like purging, laxatives, diuretics, and excessive exercise to make amends.

Bulimics suffer from impaired social and psychological functioning and from physical problems such as gastrointestinal injury due to purgatives, dental decay from regurgitated stomach acid, and even death from stomach rupture.

Regarding treatment for anorexia and bulimia, I would suggest referral to a physician for a comprehensive treatment program, as the health consequences can be very serious. I do not have specialty training in this area to offer more specific recommendations.

Time Management for Weight Loss

Let me state an obvious but often overlooked fact: having too many time commitments can make you fat.

First, when you're very busy, you have less time for meal preparation, so you end up eating fast food, which, as you know, is calorie-dense and comes in too-large portions. Second, you experience more stress when you're overextended, and this may lead you to stress-eat or to eat mindlessly. Third, you may be encumbered with unnecessary activities that prevent you from exercising.

The cure is to do what author Charles E. Hummel suggests in his books *Tyranny of the Urgent* and *Freedom from Tyranny of the Urgent*. First, determine your priorities, and then schedule your other activities around them. This will help you know which activities are optional and which are mandatory.

What should you schedule as your first priority? The answer is time with God, of course. Jesus made it clear when he gave us the first commandment that you are to love him above anything else, and that includes loving him more than your work, other people, and other things. At the minimum, this means you should read Scripture and pray regularly, as well as gather weekly with other believers for worship at church.

The second commandment says to love others as much as you love yourself (Mark 12:31). This means your next priority should be to serve those around you, probably starting with your family and working outward from there.

Voila! That is the core of your schedule. I like to think of it as *divine prioritization.*

At the very bottom of your priority list is a big group of activities that may be enjoyable but, in reality, are optional. Perhaps the list includes watching television, playing on the computer, and so forth. These are the activities you should look at cutting out to make time for your weight-loss routine.

If you feel guilty about reclaiming time for yourself (a common problem among women), then look at the second commandment backward. It says you should love yourself as much as you love other people. That means you're allowed time to take care of yourself. God said that your needs rank right up there with those of the husband, the kids, the parents, the dog, the fish, and everybody else who is to be blessed by your work on any given day.

If Junior complains when he doesn't get to do everything *he* wants anymore, remind him that he won't have anyone to wash his underwear and buy him toys if mommy and daddy die prematurely due to obesity-related diseases. It's also in the best interest of everybody in the household if you're relieved of stress through exercise. You know this is true: "If momma ain't happy, ain't nobody happy."

As you set aside time for your health, become okay with not serving everybody who wants your help. Don't feel guilty, as guilt is not of God. As Hummel points out in his book, Jesus (the only human who was ever perfectly godly) left people who wanted to be healed when he left Capernaum. He only healed the people he was supposed to heal.

Just because there are millions of good things you *could* be doing to serve God, your family, your friends, and your church, you are not necessarily *called* to do them all. It's okay to tell people, "I'm sorry; I don't have time right now. God's temple is in need of repair. I have to focus on my health." Who is going to argue with that?

Appendix C

Prayers

John 16:24 says, "Until now you have not asked for anything in my name. Ask and you will receive, and your joy will be complete." In other words, if you want to receive revelation and mental renewal from God to facilitate your weight loss, if you want to be freed from bondage to food, if you want to feel the fruit of the Spirit, then pray for those things!

I have provided these prayers as a spiritual tool to focus your heart and mind on the main themes and tasks of each chapter. Each prayer corresponds by number to the nine chapters in the book so that you can use them as you work through the book, but I have titled them thematically so that you can turn to them at any time you are struggling with a particular issue.

1. Prayer for Clarity of Mind

Heavenly Father, clear my mind of dieting and nutrition dogma that confuses and misleads me and causes me to gain weight. Fill my mind with truth. Help me to understand the best way to lose weight. Thank you for your endless mercy and grace. Amen.

2. Prayer for Godly Wisdom

Heavenly Father, clear my mind of all the myths I believe about losing weight. Take my mind off of nutrition and dieting dogma and direct me to the truth. I'm tired of being misled by worldly wisdom. I want your wisdom now. Free me from dieting bondage. Also, please speak to my heart and purify my motives for being on this plan. I want to love and respect myself as I am, and I want to lose weight to glorify you. Thank you for your mercy and love. Amen.

3. *Prayer for Eating All Food to God's Glory*

Dear Lord, show me what it means to eat to your glory, as Paul alluded to in 1 Corinthians 10:31. Help me to receive food as a special gift from you and to eat it in a way pleasing to you. Free me from guilt when I indulge in rich, delicious food, and increase my satisfaction so that I don't even want to overeat. Help me to view my self-discipline as being an offering to you, and help me to become less focused on food and more focused on you. Amen.

4. *Prayer for Tuning In to My Hunger and Fullness Signals*

Heavenly Father, I trust you. I believe you planted a tremendous capacity for healing into my body, and I need your help to find it. Help me attune to my hunger and fullness signals so I can lose weight and be a living testimony to your healing grace. Amen.

5. *Prayer for Satisfaction and Joy*

Dear Lord, help me to feel more satisfied by less food. Help me slow down when I eat. Let me savor the food and appreciate it as being a precious gift from you. Remove the distractions and guilt that rob me of my joy. Give me the discipline to stop when my hunger pangs barely go away, and then give me a sense of overflowing fullness and satisfaction in you. Thank you, Lord. Amen.

6. *Prayer for God's Strength, Power, and Discipline*

Dear Lord, please give me the strength, discipline, and desire to eat properly as an offering to you. Help me to give up the notion of willpower and rest on your power. Make this plan second nature to me so that it becomes automatic and easy. Thank you for your forgiveness and mercy. Amen.

7. *Prayer for Controlling Emotional Hungers*

Dear Lord, please help me to recognize the emotions that trigger me to eat when I'm not hungry. When you believe the time is right, help me to face those emotions directly and take control over them. Teach me to engage in healthier responses to my emotions rather than eating. Thank you, Lord. Amen.

8. *Prayer for Fighting Temptation*

Heavenly Father, please reveal to me the places, situations, and people that trigger me to eat mindlessly or in response to my sinful desires. Help me to avoid those situations where possible, and to defeat those urges when they arise. Give me strategies that will help me defeat the Enemy. Help me put the food down, midbite, if I am eating it without thinking. Please forgive me, help me forgive myself, and help me resist the urge to condemn myself over my past eating indiscretions. Thank you for your infinite mercy and forgiveness. Amen.

9. *Prayer for Perseverance*

Heavenly Father, please help me to forgive myself when I make mistakes, just as you forgive me. I know perseverance is the key to success on this journey, and I need you to help me persevere. Help me to discern why I haven't lost weight if that occurs, and give me the strength to make corrections where needed. Continue to transform my mind with right thoughts about food and eating, and help me to press on toward the goal you have set for me. Thank you, Lord. Amen.

Appendix D

Scriptural Tools

According to Luke 8:11–15, the Word of God is seed. When you plant it in the fertile, receptive soil of your mind, it transforms your thinking so that you see things more like the way God sees things so that you feel more like the way God wants you to feel and so that you act more like the way God wants you to act. The more you dwell on the Word, the more it transforms you.

Seed doesn't become fruit unless you plant it. Therefore, you must prioritize reading and meditating and praying about Scripture if you want to bear fruit in terms of losing weight.

To begin the transformation of your mind, memorize the following verses. Or write them on note cards and take them with you. When you have a free moment, look at them and meditate on them. I have listed them in the order in which they are found in the Bible.

> *My flesh and my heart may fail, but God is the strength of my heart and my portion forever.* (PSALM 73:26)

There is a way that appears to be right, but in the end it leads to death. (PROVERBS 14:12)

> *If you find honey, eat just enough—too much of it, and you will vomit.* (PROVERBS 25:16)

He who is full loathes honey, but to the hungry even what is bitter tastes sweet. (PROVERBS 27:7 NIV)

> *Blessed is the land whose king is of noble birth and whose princes eat at a proper time—for strength and not for drunkenness.* (ECCLESIASTES 10:17)

Jesus answered, "It is written: 'People do not live on bread alone, but on every word that comes from the mouth of God.'" (MATTHEW 4:4)

Blessed are those who hunger and thirst for righteousness, for they will be filled. (MATTHEW 5:6)

No one can serve two masters. Either you will hate the one and love the other, or you will be devoted to the one and despise the other. You cannot serve both God and Money. (MATTHEW 6:24)

Therefore I tell you, do not worry about your life, what you will eat or drink; or about your body, what you will wear. Is not life more important than food, and the body more important than clothes? (MATTHEW 6:25)

Come to me, all you who are weary and burdened, and I will give you rest. (MATTHEW 11:28)

What goes into your mouth does not defile you, but what comes out of your mouth, that is what defiles you. (MATTHEW 15:11)

Get behind me, Satan! You are a stumbling block to me; you do not have in mind the concerns of God, but merely human concerns. (MATTHEW 16:23)

Jesus answered, "It is written: 'Worship the Lord your God and serve him only.'" (LUKE 4:8)

Do not let your hearts be troubled. Trust in God; trust also in me. (JOHN 14:1)

Don't you know that when you offer yourselves to someone as obedient slaves, you are slaves of the one you obey—whether you are slaves to sin, which leads to death, or to obedience, which leads to righteousness? (ROMANS 6:16)

Therefore, I urge you, brothers and sisters, in view of God's mercy, to offer your bodies as a living sacrifice, holy and pleasing to God—this is true worship. Do not conform to the pattern of this world, but be transformed by the renewing of your mind. Then you will be able to test and approve what God's will is—his good, pleasing and perfect will. (ROMANS 12:1–2)

For the kingdom of God is not a matter of eating and drinking, but of righteousness, peace and joy in the Holy Spirit. (ROMANS 14:17)

> *"I have the right to do anything," you say—but not everything is beneficial.* (1 CORINTHIANS 6:12)

But food does not bring us near to God; we are no worse if we do not eat, and no better if we do. (1 CORINTHIANS 8:8)

> *No temptation has overtaken you except what is common to us all. And God is faithful; he will not let you be tempted beyond what you can bear. But when you are tempted, he will also provide a way out so that you can endure it.* (1 CORINTHIANS 10:13)

So whether you eat or drink or whatever you do, do it all for the glory of God. (1 CORINTHIANS 10:31)

> *I press on toward the goal to win the prize for which God has called me heavenward in Christ Jesus.* (PHILIPPIANS 3:14)

For, as I have often told you before and now tell you again even with tears, many live as enemies of the cross of Christ. Their destiny is destruction, their god is their stomach, and their glory is in their shame. Their mind is set on earthly things. (PHILIPPIANS 3:18–19)

> *But our citizenship is in heaven. And we eagerly await a Savior from there, the Lord Jesus Christ, who, by the power that enables him to bring everything under his control, will transform our lowly bodies so that they will be like his glorious body.* (PHILIPPIANS 3:20–21)

I know what it is to be in need, and I know what it is to have plenty. I have learned the secret of being content in any and every situation, whether well fed or hungry, whether living in plenty or in want. (PHILIPPIANS 4:12)

> *I can do all this through him who gives me strength.* (PHILIPPIANS 4:13)

Submit yourselves, then, to God. Resist the devil, and he will flee from you. (JAMES 4:7)

> *Be alert and of sober mind. Your enemy the devil prowls around like a roaring lion looking for someone to devour.* (1 PETER 5:8)

Appendix E

Eden Diet FAQs

Here are some of the questions that I have been asked about the Eden Diet. Receive the answers now so that you can build on your understanding without hindrances or misperceptions. More is written about these points within the book.

Q: **The focus of the Eden Diet is hunger pangs. Does that mean that you're supposed to feel hungry all the time on this program?**

A: *No way! You're supposed to feel hungry only right before you eat, but then eat with intense satisfaction and joy. Eating with satisfaction brings freedom from bondage so that, in time, you become less focused on food and more focused on God.*

Q: **If eating for hunger and eating for satisfaction are equally important, why does waiting for hunger get more emphasis in the book?**

A: *Waiting for hunger requires self-discipline, which is harder to learn. Eating with satisfaction involves physical pleasure, which is easier to learn.*

Q: **Why do some overweight people need to be taught how to eat with satisfaction?**

A: *If obese dieters break down and eat treats, they usually feel guilt, shame, and condemnation, and those emotions rob them of their eating joy.*

Q: **How hungry do you have to be before you eat?**

A: *You need only be hungry enough to eat an apple before you eat*

*the food you desire. This is called "The Apple Test," and the book
describes it in more detail.*

Q: **How often do you eat on this plan?**

A: *Different people prefer different eating schedules. If you want to
eat multiple tiny meals, go ahead. It's good practice so you can
learn how to identify and respond appropriately to hunger. But if
you prefer fewer larger meals, like I do, that's fine too. Just wait
until you're hungry before you eat.*

Q: **Why do some overweight people claim that they're "starving
to death" all the time?**

A: *Saying that you're "starving to death" when you're overweight
broadcasts your anxiety about going without food for only a short
time, and tells me that you may have gained weight by using food
as an emotional crutch. Remember, it is* normal *to feel hungry
before you eat!*

Q: **What if you never feel hungry?**

A: *Chances are that you have extra food stored on your body as
fat. After you lose some of your excess weight by eating smaller
portions and increasing your energy expenditure through exercise,
your hunger pangs will probably become more noticeable.*

Q: **Is the Eden Diet right for everybody?**

A: *No single diet is right for everybody. The Eden Diet is primarily
for people who wish to break free from dietary perfectionism and
focus less on food and more on God. Then, weight loss comes
secondarily and without all the stress and strain.*

Q: **What if you already eat healthy food all the time and are not
in bondage to food, eating, dieting, or body image?**

A: *I would never show up at your door and try to coerce you into
eating more junk food if you've already found peace and joy in
life and a healthy diet that works for you. But, then again, if
what you're currently doing is working, why are you reading this
book?*

Q: Won't you want to eat junk food all the time if you're allowed to eat it occasionally?

A: The opposite is true. Once you know that you're allowed treats, those foods lose their magical grip on you and you actually begin to crave healthier food more frequently.

Q: Can you eat normal serving sizes of any food and lose weight?

A: It depends on what you mean by a "normal" serving size. Sometimes what the world calls a "normal" portion is too much, especially if the food is very rich. Focus on eating slowly and eating smaller portions with more satisfaction, and the rest will fall into place.

Q: What if you require or prefer a special diet, such as a gluten-free, yeast-free, diabetic, low- salt, or vegetarian diet?

A: No matter what food you are required to or allowed to or prefer to eat, or if you are required to eat on a certain schedule, you will benefit from learning how to eat for the right reasons. The Eden Diet can be tailored to meet your personal needs and preferences.

Q: What about exercise?

A: Though exercise is not the main focus of this book, it is critical for maintaining weight loss. Do it!

Q: What is a "Christian diet"?

A: A "Christian diet" is simply a extension of the Christian lifestyle, in general. As such, it should be flexible and forgiving, rooted in God's mercy and love, and supported by prayer. A Christian diet should discourage guilt and shame and help a person experience peace, joy, love, and the other fruits of the Spirit in addition to improved physical health. I believe a Christian diet should NOT be focused on what food is right or wrong to eat, because Christ himself said in Matthew 15:11 that what comes out of a man is more important than what goes into him.

Q: Can you follow the Eden Diet if you're not Christian?

A: It depends on how you feel about Christ. If he bugs you, then maybe you should read one of the many secular (non-religious) anti-dieting weight loss books. They, too, are effective if all you want is weight loss. However, if you're not a Christian but you're open to learning more about the Lord as you lose weight, or if you seek deep emotional healing in addition to weight loss, please continue reading.

Q: What if I want to accept the Lord as my personal Savior?

A: If you want to accept the Lord as your personal Savior, say something like, "Lord, I'm sorry for my sins. Please come into my life, and help to make it all better." Or, rephrase that in a way that suits you. My own personal statement was (I'm not kidding), "Lord, whatever you think." Once you have accepted the Lord as your personal Savior, I recommend that you find and become a member of a Bible-believing Christian community.

Q: What are your religious beliefs?

A: I believe in the equality of the Trinity, in salvation through the blood of Christ, that we are saved by grace and not by our works, and that God cares more about having a relationship with us than he cares about what we do or don't eat.

Notes

Introduction

1. The Trust for America's Health and the Robert Wood Johnson Foundation, "F as in Fat 2009: How Obesity Policies are Failing America," (July 2009), http://healthyamericans.org/reports/obesity2009.

2. Cynthia L. Ogden et al., "Mean Body Weight, Height, and Body Mass Index, United States, 1960–2002," *Advance Data from Vital and Health Statistics*, US Department of Health and Human Services, Centers for Disease Control and Prevention, National Center for Health Statistics, no. 347 (October 27, 2004), 2.

3. S. Jay Olshansky et al., "A Potential Decline in Life Expectancy in the United States in the 21st Century," *New England Journal of Medicine* 352 (2005): 1138–45.

Chapter 1: Overview of the Eden Diet

1. Maxwell Maltz, *Psycho-Cybernetics* (New York: Simon and Schuster, 1960).

Chapter 2: Say Good-Bye to the Diet Mentality

1. Rena R. Wing and James O. Hill, "Successful Weight Loss Maintenance," *Annual Review of Nutrition* 21 (July 2001): 323–41.

2. Keys, A., Brozek, J., Henschel, A., Mickelsen, O., & Taylor, H. L. (1950). *The Biology of Human Starvation* (2 vols.). Minneapolis: University of Minnesota Press. Pp.832–903, as cited by David M. Garner Ph.D. *Effects of Semistarvation*, www.possibility.com/wiki/index.php?title=EffectsOfSemiStarvation.

3. Herman, C. P. & Mack, D. (1975). "Restrained and unrestrained eating." *Journal of Personality*, 43, 647-660).

4. C. Colatuoni et al., "Evidence That Intermittent, Excessive Sugar Intake Causes Endogenous Opioid Dependence," *Obesity Research* 10 (2002): 478–88.

5. Wing and Hill, "Successful Weight Loss Maintenance," 1.

6. M. R. Lowe et al., "Weight-Loss Maintenance in Overweight Individuals One to Five Years Following Successful Completion of a Commercial Weight-Loss Program," *International Journal of Obesity* 25 (2001): 325–31.

7. Michael L. Dansinger et al., "Comparison of the Atkins, Ornish, Weight Watchers and Zone Diets for Weight Loss and Heart Disease Risk Reduction," *Journal of the American Medical Association* 293 (2005): 43–53.

Chapter 3: There Is No Bad Food

1. Colatuoni et al., "Evidence That Intermittent, Excessive Sugar Intake Causes Endogenous Opioid Dependence," 1.

Chapter 4: Rediscover Your Hunger Signals

1. S. Schacter, "Obesity and Eating. Internal and External Cues Differentially Affect the Eating Behavior of Obese and Normal Subjects," *Science* 161 (1968): 751–56.

2. Lauren Lissner et al., "Dietary Fat and the Regulation of Energy Intake in Human Subjects," *American Journal of Clinical Nutrition* 46 (1987): 886–92.

3. Brian Wansink, *Mindless Eating: Why We Eat More Than We Think* (New York: Bantam-Dell, 2006).

4. P. P. Rogers et al., "Umani and Appetite: Effects of Monosodium Glutamate on Hunger and Food Intake in Human Subjects," *Physiology and Behavior* 486 (1990): 801–4.

Chapter 5: Less Food, More Joy

1. M. Livingstone et al., "Markers of the Validity of Reported Energy Intake," *Journal of Nutrition* 133, no. 3 (2003): 895–920.

Chapter 6: The Eden Diet in Action

1. M. L. Klem et al., "A Descriptive Study of Individuals Successful at Long-term Maintenance of Substantial Weight Loss," *American Journal of Clinical Nutrition* 66 (1997): 239–46.

2. B. J. Rolls et al, "Increasing the Portion Size of a Packaged Snack Increases Energy Intake in Men and Women," *Appetite* 42 (2004): 63–69.

3. N. Diliberti et al., "Increased Portion Size Leads to Increased Energy Intake in a Restaurant Meal," *Obesity Research* 12 (2004): 562–68.

4. D. A. Levitsky and T. Youn, "The More Food Young Adults Are Served, the More They Overeat," *Journal of Nutrition* 134 (2004): 2546–49.

5. S. J. Neilson and B. M. Popkin, "Patterns and Trends in Food Portion Sizes, 1977–1998," *Journal of the American Medical Association* 289 (2003): 450–53.

6. The Keystone Forum on Away-from-Home Foods: Opportunities for Preventing Weight Gain and Obesity. Final Report—May 2006, 26–28.

7. L. Young and M. Nestle, "The Contribution of Expanding Portion Sizes to the US Obesity Epidemic," *American Journal of Public Health* 92 (2002): 246–49.

Chapter 7: Feed Emotional Hunger the Right Way

1. Wing and Hill, "Successful Weight Loss Maintenance," 1.

Chapter 8: Temptation-Fighting Tools

1. Wing, Rena R. and Phelan, Suzanne. "Long-Term Weight Loss Maintenance," *American Journal of Clinical Nutrition*, Vol. 82, No. 1, 222s–225s, July 2005.

2. "The Truth about Dieting," *Consumer Reports* 67 (June 2002): 26–31.

3. J. A. Blumenthal et al., "Effects of Exercise Training on Older Patients with Major Depression," *Archives of Internal Medicine* 159 (1999): 2349–56.

4. Wansink, Brian, James E. Painter and Yeon-Kyung Lee (2006), "The Office Candy Dish: Proximity's Influence on Estimated and Actual Candy Consumption," *International Journal of Obesity*, 30:5 (May), 871–75.

5. Ibid., 85.

Additional Help

To find further support and encouragement for weight loss, please visit www.TheEdenDiet.com. The website includes numerous resources, such as links to the free Eden Diet Yahoo support group and to my blog, resources for finding or starting support groups in your geographical area, and links to past Eden Diet newsletters and online weight-loss articles.

If you are looking for additional study material, or if you suspect that there is an emotional or psychological component that underlies your eating habits, consider purchasing the *Eden Diet Workbook*. It is available at a nominal price through most bookstores and through the online store at www.TheEdenDiet.com. The workbook is essential if you intend to start or join a support group in your area.

Do you eat in response to stress, anxiety, anger, depression, or other negative emotions? If so, consider ordering the relaxing "Godly Affirmations for Weight Loss" audio CDs, which are available only through the Eden Diet website. The CDs help to relax you and fill your mind with scriptural and godly Eden Diet thoughts, which, in turn, combat those negative thoughts that sabotage your emotions and lead to overeating.

Finally, on the guestbook and questions pages of the website, you can leave a comment or ask me a question that I will do my best to answer when I'm not spending time with my family, seeing patients, or writing books!

Share Your Thoughts

With the Author: Your comments will be forwarded to the author when you send them to *zauthor@zondervan.com*.

With Zondervan: Submit your review of this book by writing to *zreview@zondervan.com*.

Free Online Resources at
www.zondervan.com

Zondervan AuthorTracker: Be notified whenever your favorite authors publish new books, go on tour, or post an update about what's happening in their lives at www.zondervan.com/authortracker.

Daily Bible Verses and Devotions: Enrich your life with daily Bible verses or devotions that help you start every morning focused on God. Visit www.zondervan.com/newsletters.

Free Email Publications: Sign up for newsletters on Christian living, academic resources, church ministry, fiction, children's resources, and more. Visit www.zondervan.com/newsletters.

Zondervan Bible Search: Find and compare Bible passages in a variety of translations at www.zondervanbiblesearch.com.

Other Benefits: Register yourself to receive online benefits like coupons and special offers, or to participate in research.

ZONDERVAN®

ZONDERVAN.com/
AUTHORTRACKER
follow your favorite authors